❋ INTO THEIR OWN ❋
• Nevada Women Emerging Into Public Life •

by
Anita Ernst Watson

A Halcyon Imprint of the
NEVADA HUMANITIES COMMITTEE

2000

❦ CONTENTS ❦

Cover photo: Special Collections, University of Nevada, Reno Library

Text Editor: Stephen Adkison
Index: Jean Stoess
Book Design: Nancy Peppin
Prepress: Reno Typographers, Inc.

© Copyright 2000
Nevada Humanities Committee
ISBN 1-890591-06-8

In 1920 Governor Emmet Boyle signed the resolution ratifying the 19th Amendment to the U.S. Constitution, an event that marked the end of a long struggle. Detail from photo, page 106 (Nevada Historical Society)

❧ DEDICATION ❧

Jean Ford was a wife, mother, and homemaker when she arrived in Nevada without fanfare in 1962. Raised to fill a traditional woman's role, Jean expected nothing more than to find a home where her husband could work as a dermatologist, her daughters could attend school, and she could enjoy a community of friends and neighbors. Fortunately for Nevada, Jean adopted her new state with open arms. First she explored it from the Strip in Las Vegas to the backroads of ghost towns, ranches, mines, and wilderness areas. She camped and hiked with her family, and she grew to love everything about Nevada, from scenic desert vistas and wildflowers to the excitement and variety of Las Vegas entertainment featuring jazz and dancing or chamber music on a Sunday afternoon.

Next Jean became involved. In discovering Nevada she saw things that needed to be improved, so she volunteered to help with projects such as preserving Red Rock Canyon as a park and creating the Clark County Library. From volunteer and citizen activist, Jean quickly moved into the Nevada legislature, serving first in the Nevada State Assembly (1972-1976) and then in the Nevada State Senate (1978-1982). Improving the legislative system intrigued Jean, and she fought for openness in government. She supported the Equal Rights Amendment, and after that was defeated, she helped introduce a variety of bills to eliminate discrimination based on sex and to create services for women in need. Those were just a few of the issues she addressed while serving in the legislature, and her interest in Nevada did not end with her final senate term.

Those who knew Jean readily recognized her many talents and skills. She was an organizer par excellence who could break a huge job into manageable tasks. She was a visionary, often recognizing a need or a possibility before others did and was always working to improve Nevada society for all of its people. She was utterly professional, thorough, and dedicated to any project she undertook. She was inclusive, always inviting others to join her endeavors. And she was an adventuress, ever-ready to accept a challenge and take a risk.

Following her days in the legislature, Jean continued traveling throughout the state and serving Nevada in many capacities from public servant and private entrepreneur to educator. In 1991 Jean temporarily filled the position of director of the Women's Studies

Program at the University of Nevada, Reno. In addition to teaching Introduction to Women's Studies, she was to teach another class of her choosing. She designed a class called, "Nevada Women on the Frontier, Past and Present" which she taught for the first time during the spring semester of 1992. Wanting each student to research in depth one woman who contributed to Nevada's history, she discovered a problem with resources. The Special Collections Department of Getchell Library was inadequate in the quality and quantity of women's collections representing the time frame and geographic area being studied.

True to form, Jean set out to improve the situation. She proposed a special project to create the Nevada Women's Archives, which was embraced by Susan Searcy, Archivist II and Bob Blesse, Head of Special Collections. With funds from Maya Miller and Barbara Thornton, a grant from the John Ben Snow Foundation, and with the support of Rollan Melton and other donors, she set in motion a project to collect papers, photographs, and information at both the Reno and Las Vegas campuses of the university. The Nevada Women's Archives now contains information on over 500 Nevada women, according to Jean.

Jean's interest in the roles women played in the history of Nevada grew along with her skills in research. Always an avid reader, she learned historic research techniques from the pros while working on a chapter in *Comstock Women, the Making of a Mining Community*. Editors of the book Ron James, Nevada's State Historic Preservation Officer, and Elizabeth Raymond, Associate Professor and Chair of the History Department at the University of Nevada, Reno, introduced her to a world of information that can be located only by serious detective work.

Her Women's Studies students continued researching women on the frontier, and Jean focused her research on the suffrage movement in Nevada. Soon her research files were bulging, and people from all over the state were contacting her about this exciting work — many wanting to help. Jean became a one-person clearing house who was capable of remembering everyone and their work on Nevada women's history projects.

Jean described the groundswell of curiosity about Nevada women in her oral history: "A lot of the interest grew when we celebrated Women's History Month in 1995, the 75th anniversary of suffrage and the League of Women Voters. We began to see what was already in the archives..., and we knew we needed to make those women come alive. I began to meet more and more people who thought that was a good idea. My telephone would ring at the Women's Studies Office, and some days I'd spend more than half my time acting as a connector for people who were interested in Nevada women's history."

The University's new Director of Women's Studies arrived four and a half years after Jean's "temporary" appointment, and by then Jean had a vision for her next mission. "I just let the Women's History Project become my baby...," she said. She drew her network of acquaintances and friends together and held brainstorming retreats. By February, 1996, Jean had co-founded the Nevada Women's History Project (NWHP), a private, non-profit organization under the umbrella of the Nevada Women's Fund. NWHP was designed to gather and disseminate information about the roles, accomplishments, and activities of Nevada women from every race, class, and ethnic background who contributed in shaping the state's destiny.

Jean described the organization's birth: "The first large membership meeting was held in January of 1996 at the Health Department Auditorium in Reno. That meeting was held in a blizzard, but we still had about sixty people in attendance. We always said we were never going to have just business meetings — that the reason we were creating a group was to enjoy coming together around Nevada women's history. We would always have some programming, so we invited the Nevada Humanities Committee Chautauqua characters and other living history performers to give a program. Everybody just got so excited...about living history as performed by those characters. January of 1996 also was the launching of the quarterly newsletter. We were so fortunate to have Sylvia Ontaneda-Bernales, who...was working on her...master's in journalism."

Since its beginning the NWHP's successes include workshops on preserving family histories and conducting research; research roundtables where members share their projects with others; outings combining hiking and history; a trip to the Bancroft Library in Berkeley for research on Nevada women; and products to sell such as a series of historic postcards, a booklet of biographies, and notepaper honoring Nevada women.

As the NWHP has evolved, the organization's mission has become more concentrated. "We now feel the major focus of the work should be toward education and teachers," Jean said. "While we enjoy doing a lot of things, the main thing is to create products that are going to get used in the schools in the future. Out of that came the Book Assessment Project, where we reviewed all the books we could get our hands on about Nevada (over 650!) to see which ones had women in them.... Out of that we published and disseminated at our annual conference a bibliography of published sources about Nevada women. It was just a simple author, title, publisher listing, but very valuable to teachers and librarians. We are...developing annotations for each of those listings and putting it on the Internet, as well as in a hard-copy form that will be extremely useful to teachers and researchers.... It also helps researchers look at what hasn't been done, so that they can move in fruitful directions.

"We got a grant to work on another project with the university to put Nevada women's biographies on the Internet. That fits right in with the mission that the legislature has given to the university's Instructional Media Services, to provide technical assistance to schools throughout Nevada so that they can make use of the Internet as an educational tool. Now the next stage is for teachers to know that it exists, so then teacher training becomes another major element of our future. We've done an in-service workshop organized by Sally Wilkins a year ago — very successful — for thirty-five teachers who taught from kindergarten through high school and showed them what materials are out there right now: what videos are available; what people perform as living history performers that just need a phone call; and how they could develop this material in the classroom for their age level.

"The web site is up and running. We have thirty-four women's biographies on it now — a brief description of their lives called 'At a Glance,' and then from two to eight or nine pages (if you were to do it in hard copy) of biography. Most of them are arranged chronologically from their early days to a listing of the accomplishments they achieved while in Nevada. They are all deceased. Our criteria were simply: we wanted at least two from every county in the state, and we wanted women who were representative of the women who have lived in those areas of the state and the kinds of work that they have done. So we have a wide range of women in the arts, mining, and ranching, in law and medicine, and in education. It isn't just about that aspect of their life; it's about their family and how they saw themselves as women if we can find that. We've tried as much as possible to include the women's own words in some aspect of the biography — excerpts from journals or diaries, letters to the editor which they wrote, speeches they gave, so...you learn about them directly through their words. The web site project will go on forever.

"It has been a wonderful organization for a lot of people who have made new friends; who have found avocations and projects; who have discovered skills they didn't know they had; who have had opportunities to lead, if they wanted that. The organization continues to be in a state of change, and there's a tremendous amount of leadership needed. We've created a success, now we need a lot of people to help continue it, and I think that will happen."

Just as Jean switched from State Chair to State Coordinator for NWHP, tragedy struck in the form of inoperable pancreatic cancer which was diagnosed in September, 1997. With it came the necessity for Jean to turn over the NWHP leadership to others.

As she was dealing with the news of her illness and making difficult decisions about how to spend her remaining time, Jean and I started to work recording her oral history for the University of Nevada Oral History Program (UNOHP). She detailed the founding of the NWHP in her oral history, *Jean Ford, A Nevada Woman Leads the Way*. Even as she was recording her oral history, Jean continued growing and learning. The best oral histories lead to new insights, and curiosity drew Jean to study her own evolution and the elements of her leadership style. She became convinced that others could accomplish as much as she. Finally, her dearest hope was that her life story would show others how to become leaders who could serve her beloved state, Nevada.

While the UNOHP committed substantial resources to Jean's oral history, the project would not have been possible without the help of several of Jean's long-time friends and supporters. Through the NWHP, funding came from Babette R. McCormick (for her son Jim McCormick) and Maya Miller. Another of Jean's friends, Joan Kerschner, director of the Nevada Department of Museums, Library and Arts, was instrumental in raising funding from the Nevada Library Association to ensure that Jean's oral history will be available in thirty libraries throughout the state.

More information about this remarkable woman's impact on Nevada may be found in her personal papers, which reside in two locations. Most papers covering her life and work prior to 1982 are archived in the Special Collections Department of the University of Nevada, Las Vegas, while papers in the Nevada Women's Archives at the University of Nevada, Reno library's Special Collections Department are primarily dated after 1982. Her papers cover a variety of issues, and finding aids are available at both locations.

Jean started her life in Nevada as wife, mother, and homemaker. Over the years she expanded her roles to include citizen activist, legislator, business woman, public figure, educator, mentor, and role model. She would tell you that Nevada made that possible, because it presented the necessary supportive atmosphere in which she could work. Those she has empowered along the way would say Jean Ford exemplified a leader, one who could both listen and fruitfully guide others. Whatever the combination, Jean is a sterling model of a woman who made history in Nevada and then worked to preserve the history of other vital Nevada women like herself.

Victoria Ford
Reno, Nevada, 1998

❊ Introduction ❊

"They cannot be *a* people without us." In an address before the Nevada Equal Suffrage Association annual convention in October 1897, Mrs. Elda Orr used those words to support her argument in favor of the enfranchisement of women. Orr's emphasis on "*a* people," with an italicized *a*, implied a vision of people that went beyond numbers and above a mere collection of bodies. Inherent in her definition of "*a* people" are the positive aspects of American culture, both the reality and the potential for greatness. According to Orr, the active participation of women, the cooperation of half of the nation's populace, was necessary to achieve that status of "*a* people" in America and in Nevada.

That phrase and that sentiment were directed specifically at the issue of women and the vote in Orr's speech. The concept of "*a* people," however, is equally applicable to the variety of venues by which women emerged into public life in Nevada in its first century of statehood. Women agitated, educated, organized, lobbied, campaigned, worked, and used virtually any means at hand to alter and improve the lives of the people of Nevada, and, not incidentally, their own lives. Not all agreed precisely what constituted improvement, but women managed to find those of like mind, or to put differences behind them in the struggle to achieve a common goal. The personalities, achievements, and activities of Nevada women as they emerged into public life form the framework of this work. And a variety of sources make up the heart of this book, and narrate the story of many of those women.

Some women of the past, particularly those who operated in the political sphere, lived relatively well documented lives. Anne Martin and Eva Adams, for example, left a wealth of public and private material. Books, manuscripts, photographs, letters, newspaper articles, and various other materials are available to study the lives and activities of Martin and Adams. It is largely due to their public position that the documentary remnants of the lives of such women have been preserved, catalogued, and made accessible for historical research.

For many other women, however, the materials that chronicle their lives have been limited, or simply unavailable. The Nevada Women's Archives, mentioned in Victoria Ford's preface to this work, have made important contributions to the lack of resources available in women's history. Other repositories throughout the state, large and small, have been building their collections of materials pertaining to Nevada women. Research projects by Jean Ford, members of the Nevada Women's History Project, state and local public agencies, and other groups and individuals, have made significant contributions to the body of historical knowledge about Nevada women. Gradually, the gaps in resources available as well as historical assessment of women's activities are being filled. This work is a result of part of that effort.

It is not the whole history of the women of Nevada. It is not even an exhaustive account of the lives and activities of Nevada women involved in the five areas of public involvement that constitute the core of this work. It is, however, a part of the picture; an overview that builds upon the research and public exhibition created by Jean Ford and staff members of some of Nevada's public history agencies. The glimpses into women's pasts are tantalizing, and they present possibilities rather than the final word on Nevada women. This is a work in progress, evidence of the diversity of women and their public roles in Nevada's past and present, as well as illustration of the variety of materials and resources that are available to document and understand that diversity.

The following text and documents focus on the public activities and roles of Nevada women in five major areas: club and civic betterment, temperance, suffrage, politics, and women working outside the home. Women in Nevada frequently found other women of like mind in one or more of the many clubs and women's groups that were organized in even the roughest and most transient communities. The clubs provided a forum for women to meet for both personal and community improvement, and, for many, facilitated the transition from the private orientation of home life into the wider realm of the public sphere.

Clubs were often created for specific reform purposes. An important focus for many Nevada public women was the effort to eradicate the outrage of alcohol in society. Temperance organizations were active from the early days of the Comstock communities. Viewing strong drink as a social pollutant, women and men worked together in the public arena to eliminate drinking and drunkenness, and thus improve the situation of the people in their own community and throughout Nevada.

Temperance groups were not the only organizations with specific purposes and goals. In the struggle to gain the vote, women argued that a fair and just government of the people should include all of the people. Mrs. Orr's speech at the 1897 convention also noted, "Men are not *the* people." She was building on three decades of effort by Nevada women, and a half century by women nationally, to obtain the right to vote. Beginning in the late 1860s, women in Nevada had declared that they had rights within the political process, as well as unique talents that would contribute to the betterment of Nevada society through the ballot box. In their view, voting women could enable Nevada citizens to be "*a* people." And they worked together toward that end.

Women had been politically active before the passage of suffrage laws, but once the vote was secured, women moved officially into the public realm of politics. And from a variety of elected platforms, Nevada women worked toward implementing reforms and legislation that would improve the lot of the citizens of the state. They united to insert themselves into the political process. Then women proceeded to use that process, through female representation, as a tool to work to improve the lives of people in Nevada.

Women, of course, did work other than that associated with the reform or betterment of society. The focus of the working woman was often confined to the betterment of her family, or aimed at finding her own fulfillment in a career or profession. Whatever the many reasons a woman worked outside the home, the workplace was another significant intersection between private and public spaces for women in Nevada. Working women were making important contributions to the making of "*a* people."

As is evident by the many activities pursued by women as they emerged into public life, the women who lived and worked in Nevada were a diverse group. Some left substantial information about themselves; many were relatively unknown. Still, their part in history added to the larger picture. A telling example of the anonymity of many women as well as the potential for furthering our understanding of the past is found in an incident in the life of Mrs. J. H. Schroeder. In October, 1914, a brief story on page eight of the *Reno Evening Gazette* described an accident in a Sparks home. Mrs. Schroeder was in the kitchen of her home, cleaning clothing with gasoline when the container exploded in her hands and ignited her clothing. Her son ran into the room and doused the flames with a blanket. Mrs. Schroeder suffered severe burns, particularly on her face and hands. The article reported that she was expected to recover.

In addition to a newsworthy story of local drama, the article provides bits of information about one woman's life in early twentieth-century Nevada. Living in the railroad town of Sparks, it's not surprising that Mr. Schroeder's employer was the Southern Pacific Railroad. Indicative of common medical practice of the period, Mrs. Schroeder was not taken to a hospital for emergency treatment; rather, a physician was called to her home to care for her. There are glimpses into Mrs. Schroeder's domestic life: she, rather than a servant, cared for the family clothing, she used gasoline to clean that clothing, and she had at least one child at home.

It might be possible to gather more information about Mrs. Schroeder. Other area newspapers might provide more information about the explosion, possibly her first name. A check of the 1910 or 1920 census, or a city directory might color in the picture a bit. Mrs. Schroeder might be listed on the membership roles of clubs or organizations in the Reno-Sparks area, or as a member of a local church. Some of her family papers might be housed in a library or historical repository. An obituary within days of the accident or years in the future could yield data about her life. And any bit of information uncovered might lead to other possibilities.

That brief article in the *Reno Evening Gazette* may well be the only public mention of Mrs. J. H. Schroeder. Like the majority of women in Nevada, she could well have lived her life in virtual anonymity, known only to her family and friends, remembered only in private as a sepia tone image in a picture album. Her experiences, thoughts, and accomplishments might never be revealed; her image and presence in the group photograph that is the history of Nevada and Nevada women might never be recognized.

That is the fate of the history of most women in Nevada, and that of most women throughout the U. S. and the world. In the past the history of women has been disregarded in favor of the more readily accessible record of the lives of famous or infamous figures, usually men, usually white. In recent decades that tradition has been changing, and more study has been devoted to the history of the silent majority of the past. Women were a significant segment of that vast, hushed company.

Such investigation requires primary sources that reveal the public and private realms of women: journals, correspondence, photographs, school report cards, business records, scrapbooks, memoirs, even furniture and clothing. Anything, in fact, that contributes to a collection of data, and leads to an understanding of the activities, motivation, thoughts and feelings of the women who have come before, the women who have left their mark, faded though it might be, on the present, is important and necessary.

The collection, identification, investigation, and study of sources and materials about women in Nevada has been one of the very significant gifts bestowed by Jean Ford and the members of the Nevada Women's History Project (NWHP). A virtual army of women and men have stormed repositories throughout the state, aided and abetted by helpful and willing curators, librarians, archivists, and staff. Jean and NWHP members have located, investigated, preserved, and disseminated many of the remnants of the past. The products of their labors have been published in books and articles, been presented as dramatic sagas around the state, been filmed as videos, and gone online.

This book is one result of that monumental effort. Jean Ford and staff members of many of the historical repositories in Nevada created an exhibit that opened in July, 1996. "Nevada Women Emerging into Public Life, 1860-1920," was displayed in the Changing Gallery at the Nevada Historical Society in Reno. The exhibit was based on research conducted in many repositories and collections throughout Nevada. For this written work, the years and the scope of women's involvement in public life were expanded. Building on the material located and evaluated by Jean and members of the Nevada Women's History Project, I conducted further research, much of it in the women's archives that she had helped to establish. Additional documents and materials were included with Jean's material, and a fifth venue of women in public life, that of work for pay outside the home, was included. This book chronicles, in text and in documentary sources, important changes experienced, and instigated, by many Nevada women.

The move into public spaces, a change experienced by diverse women in Nevada and across America, reveals important social and cultural changes for women, the family and the nation. Throughout the nineteenth century and well into the twentieth the private space of the family home was considered the ideal place for women. Women were expected to create domestic perfection within the circumscribed boundaries of their private space. Many women chafed at the cultural limits imposed on their activities. The public space was so very imperfect, and in need of women's special skills and talents.

Women expanded their boundaries by working for causes that were an extension of traditional female roles. In antebellum America, many considered the superior moral and spiritual values of women appropriate as guiding forces to help eradicate vice and immoral custom in American society. Women worked in local and national charitable organizations that nurtured the less fortunate. They rallied behind the abolitionist, temperance, and suffrage crusades.

In the decades after the Civil War and on into the twentieth century, women in Nevada echoed the national pattern of working within traditional women's roles. Often with outside help, women in Nevada expanded their boundaries. They rallied to institute reform affecting the areas that they held dear, that of the home and the family. Sometimes individually, but more often as a group, they prodded and shamed men into granting them the vote. Then they ran for elective office and created legislation to enact, force and support reform. Throughout the decades of Euro-American settlement in Nevada, women worked for pay outside the home. In short, Nevada women emerged from the domestic domain into the public sphere. The shift was generally gradual, sometimes tumultuous, and usually visible. It is that shift, that emergence which Jean Ford and her colleagues documented in their exhibit. And it is that shift which this book documents. Using the photographic images, the words, and the reports of and about the women involved, we can see a fuller, richer past.

The history of women in Nevada is by no means complete. Much of the contribution made by immigrant women, women of color, and women burdened by poverty and illiteracy, has not yet been documented. But this book represents a beginning, building upon the work and the research conducted by Jean Ford, staff at the Nevada State Museum and the Nevada Historical Society, and other historical, archival, and library personnel throughout the state, as well as the enthusiastic members of the Nevada Women's History Project.

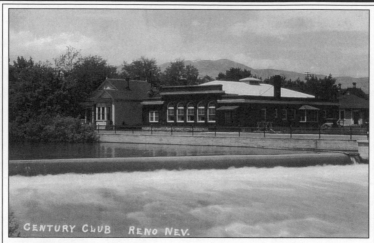

CENTURY CLUB RENO NEV.

WOMAN'S CLUB HAS COMMODIOUS QUARTERS

The first meeting of the Parents and Teachers association of the new year was held at the grammar school yesterday afternoon with good attendance. Arriving at the school house the members found the corridor a scene of interested activity, Prof. McWhinney and the most of the higher grade children busily engaged in placing the gymnastic apparatus for the girls, which has recently arrived.

Refreshments were served as usual at the social meetings of the association and a short business session held. It was reported that the board of education had granted permission to use the room formerly used for a manual training room, and the association voted to use this room for a regular meeting place hereafter. Mr. Lewis was engaged to treat its walls and woodwork to the necessary kalsomine and paint.

Each member was asked to consider herself a committee of one to extend a cordial invitation to at least five friends to attend the lecture by Mrs. Fixen on Monday night.

Established in 1894, the brick building of the Twentieth Century Club was constructed in 1925. Designed by Reno architect Fred M. Schadler, the building is listed on the National Register. (University of Nevada, Reno Special Collections)

*Activities of women's clubs were often well documented in local newspapers. (*Elko Daily Free Press, *January 10, 1914)*

CHAPTER ONE

"Social Intercourse Between Ladies of Congenial Temperament"

WOMEN'S CLUBS AND CIVIC BETTERMENT

The Twentieth Century Club still stands in Reno, a single story build-ing occupying middle ground among the parking lots and high rises that surround it. The building was constructed in 1925, a local architect's blending of the prairie style popular during the period, with classical elements that have weathered the vagaries of fashion. The Twentieth Century Club, however, is more than an old-fash-ioned relic holding its ground against the encroachment of modern Reno. It is an architectural remnant of women's past, written in brick and mortar. Organizations like the Twentieth Century Club served as a focal point for women's activities in the public sphere from the early days of Euro-American settlement in Nevada.

One enduring, and generally false, impression of the settlement of the American West is the image of stalwart settlers and rough cow-boys leaving the artificial trappings of the east behind as they fash-ioned a new life in the natural democracy of the new frontier. In fact the men and women who came west in the decades of early Nevada settlement, beginning in the 1850s, brought along cultural patterns and expectations, habits and customs of their lives elsewhere. To the extent possible, they recreated the familiar in ranching operations, businesses, and homes, in public and in private life. Beyond the walls of their homes, women duplicated their civic activities with the type of club and church work that they had been doing for genera-tions.

The late eighteenth and early nineteenth centuries were decades of tremendous change and upheaval in American culture. This tur-bulence produced both anxiety and optimism in American society. Reform movements emerged that attempted to modify the way many Americans conducted or, in the view of reformers, misspent their lives. Individuals and organizations tackled a variety of issues: sla-very, strong drink, prostitution, prisons, education, mental illness,

In the 1860s the use of state money to support a private Catholic orphanage was a controversial issue in Virginia City and beyond. Petitioners from Aurora supported the institution, which cared for children from all over the state. (Nevada State Library & Archives)

poverty, women's rights, as well as smaller crusades. A few envisioned change on a grand scale, nothing less than the whole of society, and established their own separate communities in the search for social perfection. Women were commonly perceived as the gentler sex, the nurturers and caretakers within the home. Many women built upon that image and expanded the boundaries of their domestic sphere to become the caretakers of public morality. Women were active in all of these efforts to improve society, often providing inspiration and leadership in the reform movements.

The desire to work for civic betterment was one of the customs and habits that women transported to the West. Churches had traditionally served as centers for relief and charity work, and that practice continued in early Nevada settlements. In the bustling mining cities established on the Comstock there was often a pressing need for social services. Mining accidents and injuries could, and did, leave families destitute with a disabled head of household. New widows found themselves without husband, extended family, or income to support their families. Mining strikes in other districts prompted some miners to abandon their families. In the absence of government social services, private charitable organizations at least partly filled community welfare needs. Some of the earliest relief work in Nevada was provided by members of the Roman Catholic Daughters of Charity.

Three Catholic sisters from this order, led by the intrepid Sister Frederica, traveled to Virginia City in 1864 to organize a hospital and school. Anne Butler's chapter about the Daughters of Charity in *Comstock Women*, "Mission in the Mountains: The Daughters of Charity in Virginia City," details the enormity of their task. Soon after their arrival they held a fair to raise funds for their charitable work. Money was always a problem for benevolent endeavors. The Sisters of Charity incorporated in order to qualify for state funds to build an orphanage, but the use of public money for a private institution was controversial. Although debate continued among Virginia City residents, the sisters continued to receive state funding until 1873. The Daughters of Charity remained on the Comstock until 1897, when the decline of mining activity resulted in closure of the school and hospital.

Other church denominations were also present in Nevada. A Methodist pastorate had emerged in Carson Valley by 1859. By 1861 Methodist Episcopal and Episcopal congregations had been organized

SOCIAL HOP IN GOLD HILL.—Next Thursday evening, February 9, the Ladies' Mite Society of Gold Hill will give a social hop for the benefit of Wm. J. Evans, a gentleman who is paralyzed and unable to labor. The society wish to raise money to send him to his relatives in England. Let this party and its object be remembered.

*Mite Societies, probably named for the "widow's mite" or small donation, were one of the many types of benevolent organizations that utilized the skills and energies of women in early Nevada. (*Territorial Enterprise, *February 4, 1871.)*

Relief Society Presidency in Mesquite, c. 1897
Much of the community benefit and relief work throughout Nevada was supported by church sponsored organizations such as the Relief Societies associated with the Mormon church. (Desert Valley Museum)

on the Comstock, and Presbyterians were organized the following year. There were two Jewish benevolent groups helping the Comstock communities by 1865, and a Hebrew congregation in Eureka in 1876. Lay women associated with these growing church communities arranged various fundraisers to support benevolent activities. The Ladies's Mite Society of Gold Hill and a Carson City Mite Society were raising funds by the late 1860s.

The Church of Latter Day Saints, the Mormons, were also an important and influential denomination during Nevada's settlement period. The geographical area that would become the state of Nevada was initially part of Utah Territory, and an early trading enterprise at Genoa, in Carson Valley, was established by Mormons. As part of a widespread western colonization program, members of the church established a mission in the area known as Las Vegas Spring in 1855, and groups of Mormons settled in Carson Valley and Washoe Valley the same year. Those communities were abandoned by 1857, but settlement continued in other areas. Mormon colonizers and missionaries moved to Panaca in 1864, and established colonies along the Muddy River.

Mormon women also engaged in important community and benevolent work through LDS Relief Societies. Society meetings were often devoted to religious education for the women attending, but they were also active in community work. The Relief Society in Mesquite planted and harvested cotton and cane for molasses to raise money or store credit for its members. Women in the Relief Society sat with the sick and dying, and were responsible for providing burial clothes and casket covers for the community. Maggie Pulsipher of Mesquite recalled women sewing a casket cover of bleached muslin, ribbon, and lace for Eliza Snow's burial in 1887.

The Mormon communities were small and homogenous when first settled, and the women's organizations worked within a communal structure, helping with food preservation, washing, cleaning, and responding to domestic emergencies in the communities. Like other church groups, the women of the Relief Societies raised money for missionary activity. The Relief Society in Lund, in eastern Nevada, contributed the harvest from their Victory Gardens to the war effort during the First World War. The women also collected shoes, clothing, magazines, and seeds for the needy in Europe. On the homefront they salvaged tinfoil, aluminum and waste fat, and rolled

sewing carpet rags. The
Relief Society sisters planted
cotton seed in April over
around the old Abbots Hotel.
During the summer they hoed
irrigated and cared for the
plants—often during their
regular meeting time this
work would be done. About
Oct. the cotton was picked
by the sisters, their families &
some Indians. Tables were
set out and big dinners served
for the cotton pickers. The
cotton was piled loose in
wagon boxes with high side
boards and hauled to the
factory at Washington, Utah
a three day trip where
they received 3½¢ a lb taken

in produce or credit. Some
of the cotton was ginned at
Bunkerville & hauled in bales
to Washington. The seed from
the ginned cotton was used
for cow feed. The produce received
in exchange consisted of
ready made table cloths, towels,
brooms, ax handles, butter,
home-made soap, cheese,
denims, factory linsey (a cotton
& wool material) wool flannel,
(white) grey, brown, plaids,
even bed from which came
the proverbial winter underwear
...

Maggie Pulsipher recollections
Brief handwritten snippets of memories are often significant sources of informa-
tion about the women, activities, and organizations of the past. In 1942
Maggie Pulsipher recalled early Relief Society work in Mesquite and
Bunkerville. (Desert Valley Museum)

bandages for the Red Cross.

A variety of secular benevolent organizations were also active in early Nevada. During the Civil War local societies raised money for the Sanitary Commission, a national organization supporting Union medical services. Nevada branches of the Sanitary Commission contributed more than $160,000 to the medical fund, and women were active in the fundraising. Fraternal organizations were established early in Nevada's mining and ranching communities. The Odd Fellows were organized in Virginia City by 1861, and the women's auxiliary organization, the Rebekah Lodge, was established in 1869. By 1913 there were twenty-nine Rebekah lodges throughout Nevada. The Order of Eastern Star, a women's auxiliary to the Masonic Lodge, was organized in Elko in 1879. A second chapter followed in Austin in 1882, and two more chapters were established in Carson City and Reno by 1886.

Not all women who worked for poor relief did so through large groups. In 1877 Mary McNair Mathews and Rachel Beck worked individually to alleviate hard times on the Comstock with a soup kitchen. The women gathered provisions from restaurants and vegetables and damaged packaged goods from merchants, organizing volunteers in Virginia City to feed 400 to 500 individuals for a month. They contributed their own surplus to the Sisters of Charity Orphan Asylum. Mathews, whose recollections of her time in the bustling mining town in the 1870s are a valuable source for information about a woman's life on the Comstock, was outspoken and critical of those who didn't help. The famed Bonanza Ring, for example, the renowned group of wealthy mine operators, declined to contribute.

In the later nineteenth century American women's involvement in reform efforts and clubs expanded significantly. Changes in domestic routine had created more free time for middle-class women. The availability of a wide range of commercially manufactured goods meant that women could purchase clothing items and food products that they had produced in the home in the past. Urban women shopped at the large department stores that were becoming increasingly common, and farm and small town women took advantage of catalog shopping with rural mail delivery. Domestic innovations such as electrical appliances, central heat, and hot and cold running water also freed women from some of the more arduous and time consuming tasks in the home.

LADIES' AID HALL

Friday and Saturday Nights, Dec. 1 and 2

LADIES' MINSTREL SHOW

AND

VAUDEVILLE

BENEFIT EPISCOPAL GUILD

GOLDFIELD NEWS PRINT

Goldfield Episcopal Guild entertainment
Functions sponsored by the many women's organizations in Nevada served a
variety of purposes, providing opportunities for entertainment, education,
political influence, and fund raising, as with this 1905 program. The minstrel
show was a popular form of entertainment, and the damaging racial stereotypes
were generally accepted, indicating some level of racism within the community.
(Nevada Historical Society)

The result was that many middle-class women gained more time to devote to charitable and civic occupations, and the numbers of clubs and women associated with civic groups expanded. By 1892 the General Federation of Women's Clubs linked many women's groups throughout the U. S., serving as an umbrella organization for more than 100,000 clubwomen. Women in Nevada were a part of this civic expansion. The Twentieth Century Club was founded in Reno in 1894, with the intent of providing a "broader cultivation of women and promotion of public welfare." The Twentieth Century Club became a part of the General Federation of Women's Clubs in 1897. The Leisure Hour Club in Carson City, organized in 1896, had male and female members, but a similar focus on personal development and civic improvement.

Nevada organizations had other national connections. Clara Barton established the American Red Cross in 1881. Barton had experience in organizing war relief during the Civil War, and a bureau of records in 1865 to help locate missing men. She used that experience in her work with the Red Cross. She authored an amendment to the Red Cross constitution that expanded the scope of the group's activities beyond war relief to include responses to natural disasters such as floods, earthquakes, and famine. Nellie Mighels Davis organized a Nevada Red Cross chapter in Carson City in 1899. Volunteers were active during the Spanish-American War, and have been an important part of disaster relief in the state in the twentieth century.

Women in southern Nevada were also organizing clubs and becoming involved in community and self improvement activities. In 1905, when Las Vegas was a very new community, women in the area established the Hostess Club. Members brought sewing implements to each meeting to sew for the hostess, did charitable work for the needy, and hosted an annual "Husband's Dinner" to display their culinary skills. The group was also known as the "To Help One Another" club and the "Entre Nous" club.

Mining discoveries in the Tonopah and Goldfield Mining districts around the turn of the century sparked new communities in southwestern Nevada. The arid region where the towns of Tonopah and Goldfield were established was not always a pleasant environment, and the women who settled there were hard pressed to create domestic comforts. The company of other women was welcome. By

Red Cross, Carson City
National organizations established branches in Nevada, and provided relief
work for war and other national disasters. These Carson City members of the
American Red Cross were active during the Spanish American War.
(Nevada Historical Society)

THE AMERICAN RED CROSS

RENO RED CROSS CHAPTER
91 NORTH VIRGINIA STREET
RENO, NEVADA

CHRISTMAS ROLL CALL

OFFICE, 17 NORTH VIRGINIA STREET

EXECUTIVE COMMITTEE

J. L. ROBINSON   B. D. BILLINGHURST

MRS. J. M. FULTON

Red Cross Christmas Roll Call
Like other service organizations, when it wasn't actually providing disaster
relief, the Red Cross engaged in fund raising activities.
(Nevada Historical Society)

5. ——Membership of the Waiting List——
The membership of the waiting list shall be limited to six ladies.

6. ——— Election to Membership ———
——— on the waiting list ———
The names of all of the applicants to membership of the waiting list shall be voted on at the same time, by the members of the Lunas Clava at a meeting for such purpose of which the members have been given

BY-LAWS OF THE LVNAS CLAVA
——— Object ———
The object of the club is solely to promote and facilitate social intercourse between ladies of congenial temperament.

——— Membership ———
The membership of the Lunas Clava shall be limited to seventeen members.

——— Vacancies ———
In the event of a vacancy or vacancies in the membership caused by resignation or otherwise, such vacancy may be filled by the election of a member or members of the waiting list. No one not on the waiting list may be elected a member of the Lunas Clava

——— Waiting List ———
The waiting list shall be composed of ladies who while not members of the Lunas Clava, have certain privileges. Only from this waiting list may members be elected to fill vacancies in the Lunas Clava.

BY-LAWS
OF THE
LVNAS CLAVA

Lunas Clava By-laws, 1907
The Lunas Clava Club of Tonopah, organized in 1907 "solely to promote and facilitate social intercourse between ladies of congenial temperament," was limited to seventeen members. (Nevada Historical Society)

Members of the Toiyabe Literary Club in the mining boomtown of Manhattan posed for the camera, c. 1912. (Nevada Historical Society)

Yerington Women's Club Invitation
The Yerington Women's Club was organized in 1907 for study and self-culture. They invited Governor Emmet Boyle to their annual meeting in 1915. (Nevada State Library & Archives)

Nellie Mighels Davis Like so many of the Nevada women who were publicly active, Nellie Mighels Davis, a business owner, political journalist, and founding member of several women's clubs, worked in a variety of venues. (Nevada Historical Society)

1906 the population in Goldfield was sufficiently large to support a Goldfield Women's Club. The group affiliated with the General Federation of Women's Clubs the following year.

Sam P. Davis's *History of Nevada*, published in 1913, devoted a short chapter to some of the women's clubs of Nevada. He noted that the Goldfield Women's Club was founded for the purposes of literary advancement and philanthropy, and that the members had "done much good" dispensing food and clothes in the community. Manhattan, an isolated mining town in central Nevada, had a "lively" women's organization, the Toiyabe Club, that had raised money for school play equipment and started a circulating library. Davis noted that the group began with the expressed purpose of "social pleasure and literary study," but expanded its scope to include civic improvement. He did not date the club's founding, but they were a founding member of the Nevada Federation of Women's Clubs, established in 1908. Wives of railroad men in Sparks organized the Wadsworth Club in 1909. It, too, was a social club that branched out into literary study.

Goldfield was not the only southern Nevada area that was experiencing growth. Early settlement in Las Vegas was not based on mining; rather, like Sparks, it was the result of the needs of the railroad. In 1906, Delphine Squires moved to Las Vegas with her husband, Charles, and four children. It was a new community, with most of the residents living in tents; the Squires family moved into a tent hotel until their home was built. Charles Squires was editor and publisher of the *Las Vegas Age*, the first newspaper in Las Vegas. Delphine wrote for that paper and others in the area. She had been active in club work before the move to Nevada, and continued that interest.

Women in other areas of the state also established clubs and organizations. Yerington women started a book club in 1907 under the leadership of Mrs. Della Willis Hoppin, and the Minden Fortnightly Club began as a sewing club meeting on Mrs. Joe Cardinal's porch. The women extended their concerns to civic issues and worked to improve city facilities by raising money for street lighting in Minden and the bandstand in the park.

Nellie Mighels Davis was a Carson City woman who was active in a wide variety of organizations. She came to Nevada after the Civil War with her first husband, Henry R. Mighels, who was editor

NEVADA WOMEN'S CIVIC LEAGUE
FOUNDED BY
NEVADA EQUAL FRANCHISE SOCIETY
NON-PARTISAN

STATE HEADQUARTERS
153 NORTH VIRGINIA STREET, RENO, NEVADA
WASHOE COUNTY BANK BUILDING

MEMBER NATIONAL AMERICAN WOMAN SUFFRAGE ASSOCIATION AND
INTERNATIONAL WOMAN SUFFRAGE ALLIANCE

PRESIDENT, MISS ANNE H. MARTIN, 157 HILL STREET, RENO

WHITE STATES, FULL SUFFRAGE
SHADED STATES, PARTIAL SUFFRAGE
DARK STATES, NO SUFFRAGE
NEVADA AND MONTANA WON FULL SUFFRAGE
NOVEMBER, 1914

TELEPHONE 1726

THE
WOMAN CITIZEN
A HOME JOURNAL FOR WESTERN WOMEN

Ten Cents the Copy   One Dollar the Year

MRS. GEORGE F. WEST,
President of the Nevada Federation.

NEVADA EDITION   November, 1912

Letterhead, Nevada Women's Civic League
Correspondence provides useful information about interests and activities of clubs and individuals, but sometimes the detailed letterhead is also an important historical source. This letterhead from the Nevada Women's Civic League dates from 1915. (Nevada Historical Society)

The Woman Citizen
Although publicly active in important civic projects, club work for women in the 19th and early 20th centuries was most often an extension of women's domestic and maternal roles. The photo of Mrs. George F. West and her baby underscores that perception, a 1912 version of the Madonna and Child. (Nevada Historical Society)

of the *Carson City Morning Appeal*. She worked at the paper with her husband and was the first female legislative reporter in 1877. Widowed two years later, Nellie married Sam P. Davis, whom she had hired as editor of the Carson paper. The couple bought a ranch, which Nellie managed while Sam worked at the paper. She briefly returned to reporting when she wrote up the 1897 Corbett-Fitzsimmons prize fight, fought in Carson City, for a Chicago newspaper. Nellie was one of the few women to attend the match, and she bet on Fitzsimmons.

Nellie Davis was also active in club work. Besides her work with the Red Cross, she was president of the Leisure Hour Club in 1906, and worked energetically in the planning and funding of the club house, built in 1913.

In 1908 the Twentieth Century Club called for a convention to form a State Federation of Women's Clubs. The Leisure Hour Club in Carson City, the Woman's Book Club of Yerington, and the Toiyabe Literary Club of Manhattan responded, and with the Twentieth Century Club, formed the Federation. Nellie Mighels was the first president of the politically active group. They successfully lobbied for a state law that granted equal child custody rights to mothers as well as fathers, and a bill that created a delinquent children's home in Elko. A loan fund was also on the Federation's agenda, and they provided financial support for education for girls.

Mrs. Florence Humphrey Church was president of the Federation in 1920. Like Nellie Davis, she had many interests and was active in numerous organizations and reform efforts. Educated at Oberlin College, the University of Michigan, and the University of Munich, Florence Church received her B.A. and M.A. from the University in Reno. She married Dr. James Church, a professor of classics at the University, and was a founder of the Nevada Women's Faculty Club. She served as president of the Twentieth Century Club and vice-president for both the Nevada Women's Christian Temperance Union and the Nevada Equal Suffrage League. Florence Church was closely involved in the special legislative session of 1920, which was called to ratify the 19th Amendment.

As the activities of Florence Church indicate, there were a number of clubs organized for specific reform purposes, primarily temperance and suffrage. Those groups are discussed in following chapters. Many of the general women's clubs members were active in the

EIGHTY WOMEN IN NEW SOCIETY

Voters Enfranchised at Last Election Plan Work

Eighty women, representing those of every political or non-political faith, signed the constitution yesterday of the Woman Citizens' Club and participated in the adoption of rules and by-laws and the election of officers. It is the plan of the organization to work with the civics and social science sections of the Twentieth Century Club when matters of interest to both organizations are being considered.

The object of the organization as stated in the constitution is as follows: "This shall be a non-partisan organization for the study of questions of general interest to citizens and the promotion of any movement for the betterment of society."

Any woman interested in the objects of the organization may acquire membership by signing the constitution. The dues are fixed at 50 cents a year. The officers, with chairmen of standing committees, constitute the executive board. Meetings will be held the second and fourth Wednesdays of each month. Standing committees include those on membership, house and home, program, study, outlook, legislation and law enforcement. Each committee is to consist of five members, and any member, on request, may become associated with the work of one or more committees. Meetings in the future will probably be held at the Twentieth Century Club house.

The officers chosen were: President, Mrs. Sadie D. Hurst; first vice-president, Mrs. Helen L. Belford; second vice-president, Mrs. C. H. Burke; third vice-president, Mrs. W. H. Hood; recording secretary, Mrs. Bessie Mouffee; corresponding secretary, Mrs. O. H. Mack; financial secretary, Mrs. Harold Duncan; treasurer, Mrs. Bessie R. Eichelberger; auditor, Mrs. Katherine Flett; librarian, Mrs. F. C. MacDiarmid.

Reno Evening Gazette, January 14, 1915
Once women achieved the vote, a number of women's groups worked to educate new voters. (Nevada State Library & Archives)

WOMEN'S CLUBS IN CONVENTION

Gov. Boyle and Other Distinguished Guests Speak. Vegas Women Highly Honored

(Special to The Age)

Yerington, October 30, 1915—The eighth annual convention of the Nevada State Federation of Women's Clubs met in the county court house Wednesday evening at 8 o'clock. A large audience greeted the forty-four delegates and officers present. Among the speakers for the evening were Mrs. H. S. Pohl, president of the hostess club, Mayor McDonough of Yerington, Gov. Emmet D. Boyle and Thomas C. Hart, district judge. Mrs. Charles P. Squires responded and gave the President's annual address and then presented Southern Nevada's Pioneer club women, Mrs. Helen J. Stewart, who is the guest of honor, and who responded in a few gracious words. After the formal opening of the convention a delightful social hour was enjoyed.

On Thursday afternoon the audience was charmed by the address of Mrs. Stewart, who told of many of her early experiences at the old Vegas ranch, which at that time was a resting place on the old Mormon trail. She also had a few of her beautiful Indian baskets on exhibition and in her usual pleasing manner interpreted their meaning. Mrs. Roy Martin delighted the audience with her renditions on the piano, and Mrs. C. M. McGovern, gave the report of the Mesquits club.

Mrs. Squires and Mrs. Martin were re-elected as president and corresponding secretary.

Mrs. McGovern will visit a sister in Reno before her return. Mrs. Stewart and Mrs. Squires are to be the guests of Mrs. Norcross in Carson.

Las Vegas Age, October 30, 1915
As voters, members of women's clubs became important political constituents, as evident by the mayor, governor, and district judge in attendance at a 1915 women's clubs convention in Yerington. (Las Vegas Public Library Special Collections)

OPPOSITION TO DIVORCE AND RACING HAS HEARING

Arguments Against Bills Are Presented by Committee From Women Citizens' Club of Reno

Petitions Handed in Requesting Rejection of Both Acts Signed by Residents Of This City

Special to the Gazette

CARSON CITY, Jan. 30.—In an effort to convince the senate committee on railroads and the assembly committee on public morals that the proposed race track bill and the bill restoring the six months' divorce should not pass, a delegation of Reno women, representatives of the Woman's Citizen's Club appeared before the committees yesterday. The delegation holding conference with the solons was composed of Mesdames Hood, Church, Eichelberger, Boswell, Mouffe, Parker, Nixon, Hurst, Edsall, George Taylor and Hazlett.

The railroad committee of the senate which has the race track bill under (Continued on Page Four.)

Reno Evening Gazette,
January 30, 1915
Different women's clubs frequently embraced similar political agendas and lobbied for the same causes. (Nevada State Library and Archives)

CHAPTER TWO

RM: Tell me some more about life in Gabbs during the war.

MJ: Well, the only club in town in those days was the Gabbs Women's Club. And that started in 1942 when some women had a Christmas party. They started a club and they called it the Women's Relief Club, I think. They rolled bandages and knit and did things for the war effort. But they very soon changed their name to the Gabbs Women's Club and that club is still in existence. And we started the library in 1943.

RM: Why don't you tell me about the starting of the library. I understand you know a lot about it.

MJ: Yes, I helped start it. It was started in 1943 with about 150 books which were given to us by the USO Club in Reno. We've had many, many homes but the company finally gave us the building where we are right now.

RM: Could you tell me where the building is?

MJ: It's right across from the school at 602 3rd Street.

RM: It's across the street from the school?

MJ: Yes, from the new gymnasium. It used to be the townsite office. They collected the rents and the water and lights and everything there. They gave us that building and we were really outgrowing it, so when Mrs. Gates – Barbara Gates, wh[...] away (she was the wife of [...] memorial donations. And [...] see if we can build a roo[...] volunteer help. Basic In[...] and we built this room an[...]

Margaret Jones Oral History
Oral histories provide information about the more recent past. Margaret Jones remembers club work in Gabbs during the Second World War as well as the beginnings of the town library. (Nye County Town History Project)

WELLS HIGH SCHOOL

HOWARD WESTERVELT PRINCIPAL   WELLS, NEVADA   H. H. CAZIER BOARD MEMBER

April 11, 1931.

Mrs. Charles Priest,
Carson City,
Nevada.

Dear Mrs. Priest:
Mr. Westervelt gave me your letter concerning the essays, this morning, and I am very sorry that it was necessary for you to go to so much trouble.
Through a misunderstanding of the rules of the contest, we chose the best essays of each title, rather than of each group.
The best essays in Groups I and II, however, are:
"The Story of my Grandmother"– Merlyn Harney
"The Story of my Grandfather"– Robert Gulley
"An Old settler's Story"– Lafe Leach.
"Historic Landmarks" – John Franklin
"Historic Landmarks" – Raymond Gray
"Historic Landmarks"– Kathryn Hartleigh.
I am very sorry that we have inconvenienced you by this misunderstanding.
Sincerely,
Theo. Almstead
English Instructor
Wells High School.

Letter to Mrs. Charles Priest
Mrs. Charles Priest was president of the Nevada Federation of Women's Clubs in 1931 when she received this letter regarding an essay contest sponsored by the Federation. (University of Nevada, Reno Special Collections)

suffrage movement, but the women's clubs were more focused on wider issues of civic improvement and reform rather than the problem of their members' lack of voting rights. The national umbrella agency of women's groups, the General Federation of Women's Clubs, did not officially endorse women's suffrage until 1914, when the battle was almost won. The Nevada Federation of Women's Clubs came out in support of suffrage that same year, when the amendment to the Nevada constitution, granting women the vote, was finally passed.

When women achieved the vote, several organizations focused on turning the new voters into good citizens. In 1915 the Nevada Equal Franchise Society, its purpose fulfilled, shifted gears and became the Nevada Women's Civic League. That year, the February 20th issue of the *Clark County Review* reported on the organization of the Las Vegas Civic League with thirty-four charter members. The women, according to the newspaper, would meet twice a month to "study civic, social, political, city, county and state government affairs for their general education and with the especial purpose in view of learning to vote as intelligently as possible when their opportunity arrives." The League of Women Voters was organized in 1919, during a visit to Nevada by Carrie Chapman Catt, specifically to educate women about their political responsibilities and the wise use of the ballot box.

The League went beyond their original mandate, however, in the cause of civic reform. In 1922 the organization launched an anti-prostitution crusade that resulted in a Reno city ordinance forbidding brothels. Prostitution was an important issue in the city elections the following year. Unfortunately for the women reformers, E. E. Roberts, who wanted a wide-open town, became Reno's mayor. In January 1923 the city council passed an ordinance that established a red-light district along the Truckee River that would become famous as the Stockade. On this issue, the moral reform effort launched by the League of Women Voters enjoyed only limited and brief success.

Women continued to organize over the decades of the twentieth century. In her oral history, Margaret Jones recalled a Christmas party in Gabbs in 1942 when local women started a club. First known as the Women's Relief Club, they contributed to the war effort by rolling bandages and knitting. The club name was changed shortly after its founding, and the Gabbs Women's Club is still active.

Yerington, Nevada,
Feb. 1, 1916

Gov. Emmett Boyle,
Carson City, Nevada

Dear Gov. Boyle:

The Home Economics, Conservation and Public Health Departments of the Nevada Federation of Women's Clubs are co-operating with the Children's Bureau, U.S. Department of Labor and the General Federation of Women's Clubs in the celebration of Baby Week, March fourth to eleventh. Our purpose is to fix the attention of the whole state, especially during that week, upon the proper care of babies, particularly during the summer months, in order to further reduce infant mortality.

We believe that much good might be done to spread the influence of this campaign in towns having no women's club if you officially declared the week March 4 to 11, Baby Week in Nevada.

Thanking you in advance, and trusting the success of this campaign may be [____], I am,

Sincerely,
Edith West, Chr.

Letter to Boyle, 1916
Public information about women often listed them by their formal married name, and can make it difficult to identify specific women. The signature of Edith West on this letter to Governor Boyle provides a bit more information about Mrs. George F. West. (Nevada State Library & Archives Boyle files)

The women's clubs, nationally and in Nevada, were primarily organized and peopled by middle-class Euro-American women, the economic and social class that had the financial resources and leisure time to volunteer for the variety of civic projects the clubs supported. Working class women and women of color tended to be the recipients of club benevolence rather than members of the organizations. The General Federation of Women's Clubs denied an African-American woman a delegate seat at the national convention in 1900, and denied its own progressive and democratic sentiments, perhaps largely in the interests of appeasing southern club women.

Historical research into the public and private lives of women of color in Nevada has barely scratched the surface, but the contributions of committed women are gradually coming to light. Lubertha Johnson, was the first African-American nurse in southern Nevada. An African-American woman and granddaughter of a slave, she was born in Mississippi and spent her young adulthood in Chicago. She moved to Las Vegas in the early 1940s. A member of Gamma Phi Delta Sorority, Johnson was not a member of any of the other women's clubs and organizations just discussed. Twice president of the NAACP in Las Vegas, she was dedicated to civic improvement and reform. Johnson worked independently to effect change by lobbying lawmakers and powerful people, and was credited during her lifetime for her contribution to open housing legislation, and the passage of civil rights legislation in Nevada.

Johnson encountered the bias that was so prevalent in the America of her youth, particularly in the South. When her family began the move north, Southern racial restrictions were apparent when they were refused service at the local train station. The family was forced to move on to another town to purchase their tickets for the train ride to Chicago. Johnson worked for change, however, in a public sphere that could be hateful, pursuing the reform ideal embraced by many club women in Nevada without the structure and backing of the clubs that had been so important to her Euro-American contemporaries.

Groups for women of color were organized in Nevada. The Negro Business and Professional Women's Association was established nationally in New York in 1935, and a local chapter started in Reno in 1972. In more recent decades, women of color have become members of groups that were previously restricted to Euro-American

Lubertha Johnson worked to improve the lives of African-Americans. She was twice president of the NAACP in Las Vegas. (University of Nevada Oral History Program)

Mrs. Delphine Squires, wife of the editor of the Las Vegas Age, was also involved in the newspaper business and women's clubs. She was an active campaigner in southern Nevada for women's suffrage. (Nevada Historical Society)

NEVADA FEDERATION OF WOMEN'S CLUBS. PRESIDENTS.		
YEAR.	NAMES.	RESIDENCE.
1908-1910	Mrs. Saml. P. Davis.	Carson City
1910-1911	Mrs. O. H. Mack	Reno
1911-1913	Mrs. Geo. West	Yerington
1913-1914	Mrs. Fanny G. Patrick	Reno
1914-1916	Mrs. C.P.Squires	Las Vegas
1916-1919	Mrs. Pearis b. Ellis	Carson City
1919-1921	Mrs. J.E. Church	Reno
1921-1923	Mrs. Wm. Dent Mason	Elko
1923-1927	Mrs. D.E.Ericson	Reno
1927-1931	Mrs. C.C.Taylor	Carson City
1931-1934	Mrs. Geo. Willis	Yerington
1934-1937	Mrs. E.E.Ennor	Elko
1937-1940	Mrs.O.G. Purdy	Sparks
1940-1942	Mrs. A.C.Grant	Las Vegas
1942-1944	Miss Felice Cohn	Reno
1944-1946	Mrs. Hazel B. Denton	Caliente
1946-1948	Mrs. Leon Mack	Reno
1948-1950	Mrs. H.L.Bruce	Elko
1950-	Mrs. Isabelle Blackman	Las Vegas

Delphine Squires's 1951 history of club work provides a glimpse of the isolated life that many women lived in a rugged landscape, as well as detailing names and dates of presidents of the Nevada Federation of Women's Clubs. (University of Nevada Las Vegas Special Collections)

women. As churches have integrated, women of color have become a part of women's societies associated with various denominations.

In 1951, nearly a half century after she first came to Las Vegas, and after an equal number of years of club involvement, Delphine Squires reflected on the significance of women's clubs in Nevada. Recalling the difficulties that women faced in a sparsely populated state, with daunting transportation challenges, she asserted, "we Nevada women feel that we have accomplished a great deal." There was much to be done:

> We needed trees and other kinds of vegetation, but first we had to develop water; we needed highways, better housing, better schools, churches, libraries, sanitation—these were the things we worked for and these are the things we have helped to acquire.

Many women and many groups working toward a general concept of civic reform and betterment "helped to acquire" those things. The reform impetus that motivated women to move beyond their domestic space, a comfortable place that the majority of women and members of society believed was a woman's rightful place, was a powerful force. Most of the women who worked through various organizations aimed at civic improvement were firmly and sincerely convinced that the reforms that they were attempting to make would result in personal and social uplift. The money they raised for those less fortunate, the books they purchased for libraries or read and discussed among themselves, even the trees they planted—all were understood to be effective tools for social improvement. Most were sincerely dedicated to their vision of civic betterment, and they targeted many issues and individuals.

Several of the reform goals that were a part of the general effort to improve society were sufficiently problematic to warrant a reform movement of their own. Such was the case with the temperance movement, and the struggle to gain suffrage for women. Both are dominant themes in the public work of the women of Nevada and throughout the nation.

Bars and saloons were a common sight in Nevada communities. (University of Nevada, Reno Special Collections)

PROCEEDINGS

OF THE

TEMPERANCE CONVENTION.

FORMATION OF THE

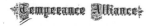

OF THE

STATES OF CALIFORNIA AND NEVADA.

HELD IN SAN FRANCISCO, APRIL 2, 1873.

SACRAMENTO:
RECORD STEAM BOOK AND JOB PRINTING HOUSE.
1873.

*The movement to repress drinking in American society had long been a national issue.
(Nevada Historical Society)*

WOMEN AND TEMPERANCE IN NEVADA

The letterhead from the Nevada Woman's Christian Temperance Union in the early twentieth century provides revealing insights into the intent and the motivation of the group. Above its name is a quote from I Corinthians 10:24, "Let No Man Seek His Own, but Each His Neighbor's Good." The watchword, "Agitate, Educate, Organize," and the Bible verse highlight the resolve and reveal the impetus of the Temperance movement in Nevada, a reform movement dating from the earliest periods of Euro-American settlement in Nevada. Temperance aimed to reform and improve Nevada society by agitating, educating, and organizing. Temperance crusaders looked out for the good of their neighbors by eliminating the threat that they believed strong drink posed to individuals and to families. A variety of groups worked to those ends in Nevada for more than a century.

Henry Blasdel, Nevada's first governor, and his wife, Sarah Cox Blasdel, championed the temperance cause. During Blasdel's tenure, 1864 to 1871, liquor was banned at gubernatorial functions. Blasdel was referred to as "the coffee and chocolate governor," a full decade before President Rutherford and "Lemonade Lucy" Hayes promoted temperance in the White House.

The Blasdels's support of temperance was an informal, if highly public, declaration of their sentiments. More structured support was found in weekly meetings of the Sons and Daughters of Temperance. The members of the temperance group faced a daunting challenge; the Comstock communities had numerous retail and wholesale liquor establishments and several breweries. Mary McNair Mathews, a widow who came west from New York to Virginia City in 1869, wrote in great detail of her experiences living and working on the Comstock. Her memoirs, *Ten Years in Nevada*, provide a rich source of information about a woman's life in a Nevada mining community, and document the activities of a woman who frequently crossed the boundaries between private and public spheres. A woman of strong convictions, Mathews was an enthusiastic temperance worker, and was proud of the money that she raised through "entertainments" for support of the movement. She asserted, "the temperance people worked very hard to get laws passed at the assembly by sending mammoth petitions." Mathews collected names for the petitions at the post office and by standing in front of her house, twice a day for two weeks. She boasted of her high numbers of signatures for the cause.

The men and women who drank, as well as those who worked to eliminate intemperance in early Nevada, were building on long-held traditions and patterns in American culture. Drinking had been a part of social, political, and economic life from earliest times. In public houses, saloons, taverns, and inns, Americans conducted business, argued politics, and celebrated significant events over a drink. In urban settings, it was not uncommon to send small children to a local saloon with a bucket (the edge was coated with petroleum jelly or oil to keep the foam down) to buy beer for the family meal. Drinking alcoholic beverages could spring from health concerns. In both rural and urban areas it was often safer to drink a fermented beverage than to drink the water.

Not all observers, however, approved of such choices. There were scattered protests against drunkenness in the late eighteenth century, primarily from religious groups such as the Quakers and the Methodists, which would remain ardent supporters of temperance. Dr. Benjamin Rush, a well known physician of the period, published a tract in 1784 that advised moderation with intoxicants, and some groups advocating moderation organized in the late eighteenth and early nineteenth centuries. By the 1820s a growing reform element was calling for the elimination of all spirits, in contrast to those who promoted moderation or who objected only to drunkenness and did not condemn drinking. The Reverend Lyman Beecher was using his pulpit to preach against drinking, and in the fall of 1825 delivered a series of six sermons warning of the evils of strong drink.

The reform impetus grew and by the 1830s temperance organizers were depicting drunkenness as both a social and a spiritual evil. The American Temperance Union and the Washington Temperance Society worked to bring the anti-drinking message to Americans in the years before the Civil War. The church based groups were joined by secular associations, and the initial approach of moral suasion gave way to efforts to legislate social change. The Sons of Temperance, the group that attracted Mary McNair Mathews's participation, was established in 1843, and became an important non-sectarian temperance organization.

The efforts of Virginia City's temperance-oriented citizens, then, were part of a larger national movement. An organizational meeting of the Temperance Alliance of California and Nevada was held in April 1873 at the YMCA Hall in San Francisco. The Reverend T. H. McGrath, a Methodist minister who had addressed a Sons and Daughters of Temperance meeting in Virginia City several years earlier, attended the meeting. Mrs. Carrie Young of Ophir was a speaker at the San Francisco gathering, and addressed the question, "What is the best mode of presenting Temperance principles to our children?"

While regional groups were organizing, national temperance organizations continued the battle against the bottle. In 1874, the National Women's Christian Temperance Union was established in Cleveland, Ohio. Hundreds of thousands of women joined the WCTU, a truly national organization for women. Frances Willard, who was corresponding secretary when the WCTU was started, became president in 1879. Under her leadership, the WCTU effected important social change. While temperance was the focus of Willard and the organization, she was interested in any improvement in the lives of women and children. The WCTU campaigned for prison reform, labor laws to protect women and children, and suffrage.

An important goal of the suffrage crusade was legislation to gain the vote for women in order to help enact anti-liquor legislation. That dedicated political agenda earned the enmity of powerful liquor interests, and the liquor lobby worked against temperance and suffrage for the next fifty years.

Temperance activity continued as a significant aspect of women's public life in Nevada. Sallie Hart, who was billed as "the little Temperance heroine," was featured at the National Guard Hall in Virginia City in 1875, where she delivered a lecture on the life of philosopher and critic Margaret Fuller. The following year the *Humboldt Register* reported temperance meetings, with good attendance, in Winnemucca. According to a 1910 history of the Nevada WCTU, at least two temperance groups antedated the WCTU in Reno. There are no dates in the account of the groups. One, called the Reform

This late 19th-century poster featured Frances Willard, national leader of the temperance movement. (Nevada Historical Society)

Club, had dissolved but its members had reorganized into the Women's Temperance Union. The outline of WCTU work in the east was brought to Reno by a Mrs. De La Matyr and the existing union adopted the name and work of the WCTU in 1882.

As they would on behalf of Nevada suffrage activities, national leaders visited the state to help organize and to stimulate interest in the temperance cause. Frances Willard embarked on a tour of all states in 1883 (there were thirty-eight at the time) with Anna Gordon. Willard and Gordon led the organizational meeting, held at the Reno Methodist Church, to establish the Nevada WCTU. Mrs. H. Elizabeth Webster was elected president, and Miss H. K. Clapp was corresponding secretary. The first state convention was held in Reno in 1885.

By 1888 there were fifteen unions active in Nevada. Those unions helped to defeat a lottery bill that year. Lucy Van Deventer had been elected state president in 1887, and held that position for most of the decade following. Married to Eugene Van Deventer, a circuit-riding Methodist minister in northern Nevada, Lucy Van Deventer was involved in a number of reform causes, with a particular affinity for efforts to provide protection to women and girls. She labeled the indignities forced upon little girls "the shame of our boasted civilization." Her concerns dovetailed with the activities of the Nevada WCTU. As part of the effort to educate, temperance reformers endeavored to reach out to the youth of the state. Two hundred young people, boys and girls, were organized into Loyal Temperance Legions.

That same year, the *Nevada Prohibitionist* commenced publication in Genoa, Nevada, initially under the leadership of Mrs. M. E. Latta and the Reverend C. H. Gardner. Proclaiming itself the official organ of the WCTU, the newspaper was "devoted to the work of creating public sentiment against the evils of intemperance and in favor of pure homes, society, and politics." The publication lasted for only one year.

Temperance advocates, however, were busy throughout the 1890s. The Reno union purchased a lot on the corner of 2nd and West streets in Reno in 1890, designated as the site for a state headquarters. In 1891 the Nevada WCTU petitioned the legislature in support of suffrage. Temperance in Nevada had long been associated with the suffrage movement: in 1870 the Sons and Daughters of Temperance sponsored a debate on women's rights in Virginia City.

Reno Nev Oct 17th 1893

The regular meeting of the W. C. T. U. was held on the above date at the residence of Mrs. M. J. Cook

Devotional exercises were led by the President Mrs Cook who read the 127th Psalm

Mrs Simms offered prayer

Officers absent Mrs Westlake Mrs Fitzgerald Mrs Show and Mrs Blandel 1st 2d 3d and 4th Vice Presidents

Minutes of former meeting read and approved

The treasurer reported having paid S Emerich 3.00 for House Lining

It was ordered that the committee on Medal contest work borrow funds from the tablet fund to start with

Mrs Gilman reported having seen Professor Pray in regard to the pupils of the High school writing Essays on Narcotics

It was voted to sell the house lining to Pugh & Cook also sell the bunting

Dues 60 cents

Adjourned to meet in two weeks at the Residence of Mrs M. J. Cook

Mary A. Boyd Rec Sec

Nevada temperance supporters organized in 1883 when Frances Willard visited the state. This Reno branch was meeting every two weeks in the homes of members. (Nevada Historical Society)

The Nevada Prohibitionst.

VOL. II.   GENOA, NEVADA, APRIL 1 1889.   NO. 4.

The Nevada Prohibitionist was "Devoted to the work of creating public sentiment against the evils of intemperance and in favor of pure homes, society, and politics". (Nevada Historical Society)

NATIONAL
WOMAN'S CHRISTIAN TEMPERANCE UNION

PHYSICAL CULTURE DEPARTMENT.
LEAFLET No. I.

A New Field for Educators.

BERTHA MORRIS SMITH, B. E.

The time is fast approaching, if indeed it is not already here, when educators and thoughtful people generally, who are seeking for the means whereby a higher type of man upon the earth may be evolved, will recognize the fact that our present educational system does not come up to its highest possibilities, because it neglects to provide for the harmonious development of all the faculties.

The educational methods most commonly in vogue seem to regard man as a dual being, made up of mental and bodily parts, that have very little more in common than house and tenant, and consequently the body receives only such attention as is required to keep it in a condition fit for the habitation of the mind.

The maxim that a sound, clear mind must have a sound body in which to dwell, however old and often demonstrated, does not seem to have gained the recognition necessary to secure the practical application of bodily training in the schools of our country.

One of the greatest mistakes of our educational system, is that it imposes tasks upon children that involve a constant expenditure of nervous energy five hours in a day and five days in a week, and in no way makes provision to assist nature in her attempts to repair this waste. The result of this inverted order of teaching and the unnatural demand for mental

Morality and a healthy, physically fit lifestyle were considered a natural alliance in the view of temperance advocates. (Nevada Historical Society)

The burning of whiskey barrels warmed the hearts of anti-drinking enthusiasts in Carson City in 1909. (Nevada Historical Society)

(copied)

A short sketch of the W.C.T.U. work in Nevada.

This work was begun in Reno. There had been a temperance club, composed of both men and women, called the Reform Club. When this was dissolved, the women who had been its members, formed an association called the Women's Temperance Union. In 1882 Mrs De La Matyr came to Reno and brought an outline of the W.C.T.U. work in the eastern states. The union then decided to adopt the name and the work of the W.C.T.U. In May, 1883, Miss Willard visited this State and organized unions in Carson and Virginia City, and also organized the State Union, with Mrs Wm Webster as president. Mrs Eliza Boardman, recording secretary, Miss H. K. Clapp, corresponding secretary, and Mrs Eliza Waggoner, treasurer.

The first State Convention was held in Reno, Sep. 29. 1885. The same officers were elected except the treasurer. Mrs Flora M. Helm was elected treasurer and Mrs M.S. Bonni-field, vice president-at-large, and ten superintendents. Mrs. Cooley, national organizer, was present.

The second convention was held in Carson, April 4. 1887. Mrs Van Deventer was elected president. Mrs Boyd and Mrs. Flint - vice-presidents, Miss Eva Barnes, recording secretary. Mrs F. M. Helm, corresponding sec. & Mrs F.J. Crawford, treasurer. Constitution was drawn up and adopted. Miss Esther Pugh was present. She was National treasurer.

Third convention met at Reno, June 19. 1888. Mrs Van Deventer was re-elected president - Mrs Frances Mc. Evers, recording secretary. Mrs C.B. Norcross, cor. sec. and Mrs Crawford - treasurer. Miss C.S. Burnett was present, 14 unions reported. I have not been able to find any information in regard to the Fourth and Fifth conventions.

A short history of the Women's Christian Temperance Union was handwritten in 1910. (Nevada Historical Society)

And many of the women active in temperance, both as leaders and as members, were also involved in efforts to gain the vote for women.

Annual conventions were held, and at the tenth convention, in 1895, Dr. Eliza Cook of Mottsville was elected president. Like so many other women who made significant contributions to social welfare, Dr. Cook did not limit her attention or her energies. She also took an active leadership role in the Nevada Equal Suffrage League. The Nevada unions maintained relations with national organizations and in 1899, Mrs. Flora McRae was the first Nevada delegate sent to the national WCTU convention in Seattle; other delegates attended in subsequent years.

By 1910, the short history of the Nevada WCTU listed unions in Reno, Susanville, Carson, Virginia, Gold Hill, Genoa, Sheridan, Mason Valley, Elko, Winnemucca, Wadsworth, Lovelock, Ruby Hill, Eureka, and Tuscarora. It was an impressive representation of organization within the state. Apparently, however, organization did not necessarily denote activity. The author of the history both lamented the inaction and offered hope for the future: "Many of the unions are now sleeping but the voice of a leader in each would arouse them, and the united and persevering work of 15 unions would certainly enable Nevada to arise and shake off the crushing weight of the saloon and take her place among the states with a population equal to any of them."

The Anti-Saloon League held a convention in Reno in 1910, where Mrs. Nettie Hershiser, president of the Nevada WCTU presented her thoughts on "The Outlook." During the first two decades of the twentieth century, the prospects for many reform efforts were promising. With sincere concern for public welfare, women were attempting to clean up prisons and factories, rehabilitate prostitutes, establish libraries and parks, protect laboring women and children, and much more. Nevada women were part of a sweeping national effort to transform American society. Strong drink was one vice that women persistently attacked.

The Nevada WCTU continued to attack through education of young people. A young WCTU club was organized at the University of Nevada in 1912 by Mrs. Alice Elder. Essay contests were sponsored in schools, and temperance literature was distributed through Sunday schools. Reform activity by temperance supporters expanded beyond the scope of strong drink. An honorary member of the Nevada WCTU

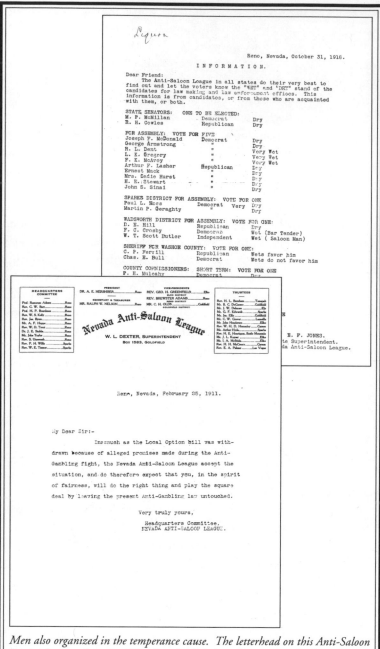

Liquor

Reno, Nevada, October 31, 1918.

I N F O R M A T I O N.

Dear Friend:

The Anti-Saloon League in all states do their very best to find out and let the voters know the "WET" and "DRY" stand of the candidates for law making and law enforcement offices. This information is from candidates, or from those who are acquainted with them, or both.

STATE SENATORS: ONE TO BE SELECTED:

| M. P. McMillan | Democrat | Dry |
| R. H. Cowles | Republican | Dry |

FOR ASSEMBLY: VOTE FOR FIVE

Joseph F. McDonald	Democrat	Dry
George Armstrong	"	Dry
R. L. Dent	"	Very Wet
L. K. Gregory	"	Very Wet
F. K. McAvoy	"	Very Wet
Arthur F. Lasher	Republican	Dry
Ernest Mack	"	Dry
Mrs. Sadie Hurst	"	Dry
H. E. Stewart	"	Dry
John S. Sinai	"	Dry

SPARKS DISTRICT FOR ASSEMBLY: VOTE FOR ONE

| Paul L. Ross | Democrat | Very | Dry |
| Martin P. Geraghty | | | Dry |

WADSWORTH DISTRICT FOR ASSEMBLY: VOTE FOR ONE:

D. E. Hill	Republican	Dry
F. C. Crosby	Democrat	Wet (Bar Tender)
W. T. Scott Butler	Independent	Wet (Saloon Man)

SHERIFF FOR WASHOE COUNTY: VOTE FOR ONE:

| C. P. Ferrill | Republican | Wets favor him |
| Chas. E. Bull | Democrat | Wets do not favor him |

COUNTY COMMISSIONERS: SHORT TERM: VOTE FOR ONE

| P. H. Mulcahy | Democrat | Dry |

E. F. JONES.
te Superintendent.
da Anti-Saloon League.

Reno, Nevada, February 25, 1911.

My Dear Sir:-

Inasmuch as the Local Option bill was withdrawn because of alleged promises made during the Anti-Gambling fight, the Nevada Anti-Saloon League accept the situation, and do therefore expect that you, in the spirit of fairness, will do the right thing and play the square deal by leaving the present Anti-Gambling law untouched.

Very truly yours,

Headquarters Committee,
NEVADA ANTI-SALOON LEAGUE.

Men also organized in the temperance cause. The letterhead on this Anti-Saloon League letter, written in 1911, lists the church and community leaders who were involved. In 1918 the League was providing information about the stand that candidates were taking on the liquor issue. (Nevada Historical Society)

PROVISIONAL PROGRAM

FOR THE

State Convention of the Nevada Anti-Saloon League held in Reno, May 6th to 8th, 1910.

Friday   8:00 P. M.—Devotional Service led by Rev. C. L. Mears, Reno.
          8:20 P. M.—Address of Welcome, Rev. Jas. Byers, Reno.
          Response, Rev. W. H. D. Hornaday, Carson.
          8:45 P. M.—Some Impressions of Nevada and Its Needs,
          Rev. S. A. Thompson, Supt. Methodist
          Missions.
          Appointment of Committees.

Saturday 9:30 A. M.—Devotional Service led by Rev. L. L. Tower,
          Carson.
          Special Prayer for the Movement.
          10:00 A. M.—The Status of the Liquor Traffic in Nevada,
          Judge C. E. Mack, Reno.
          10:20 A. M.—Discussion.
          10:30 A. M.—The Anti-Saloon League, Its Work and Methods,
          Superintendent.
          11:00 A. M.—The Outlook, Mrs. Nettie P. Hershiser, President,
          Nevada, W. C. T. U.
          11:20 A. M.—Local Option or High License, Which? Rev. S. G.
          Wilson, Sparks.
          11:40 A. M.—Discussion led by Rev. L. M. Burwell, Reno.
          12:00   M.—Adjournment.
          1:30 P. M.—President's Address.
          1:50 P. M.—The Local Situation in the Various Parts of the
          State, by delegates present.
          2:15 P. M.—Business   Session:
          Report of Superintendent,
          Report of Secretary and Treasurer,
          Reports of Committees.
          3:15 P. M.—The First Move, Rev. H. E. Henriques, Battle
          Mountain.
          3:35 P. M.—General Discussion.
          4:00 P. M.—The Direct Primary Law; How It Will Help Us.
          Adjournment.
          8:00 P. M.—Devotional Service, led by Rev. G. W. Beatty,
          Yerington.
          8:20 P. M.—Address, Rev. H. H. McCreery, Carson.

Sunday   3:00 P. M.—Men's Meeting, addressed by different speakers
          present.
          8:00 P. M.—Devotional Service, Rev. Mark White, Lovelock.
          8:20 P. M.—Mass-Meeting, addressed by Rev. A. C. Bane,
          D. D., Supt. California Anti-Saloon League.

                                                    ⎧ W. L. Dexter
                                    Committee   ⎨ C. L. Mears
                                                    ⎩ L. M. Burwell

*Provisional Program The Anti-Saloon League held a convention in Reno in
1910. (Nevada Historical Society)*

The Nevada WCTU had branches throughout the state. These Goldfield temperance advocates lined up for the photographer. (Nevada Historical Society)

formed anti-cigarette leagues for boys (smoking was not commonplace for girls) in Reno, Sparks, Fallon, and Elko in 1914.

The WCTU also lobbied for uniform divorce laws. Each state determined its own requirements to obtain divorce, and some were more liberal than others. Nevada was among the most liberal with a short residency requirement and lenient grounds for divorce. A proposed federal uniform divorce law would have resulted in identical and more stringent requirements for divorce throughout the nation, but Progressive reformers never succeeded in passing such a law.

Social issues like temperance and suffrage were the platforms from which reform efforts were launched, but a wide variety of social ills caught the attention of the women seeking to improve the status and living conditions of women and the family. In their efforts on behalf of purity in American society, temperance groups also supported an anti-polygamy amendment, as well as efforts to abolish legalized boxing, to suppress the white slave trade, and to make gambling illegal. The temperate "coffee and chocolate governor," Henry Blasdel, had also resisted gambling, and vetoed an 1867 bill legalizing gambling. He lost his fight when gambling was legalized in 1869. In his work, *History of Nevada*, Russell Elliott has observed that, in the reform enthusiasm of the Progressive period of the early twentieth century, the fight for social virtue on this front did prevail and gambling was again outlawed in 1910. Reform victories in Nevada, however, could be transitory. Some card games were legalized in 1911; then in 1913, all gambling was again outlawed. In 1915 card games, those where the deal alternated, were once more legal. Of course, in 1931, all gambling was once again legalized and the course of life in Nevada was irrevocably altered.

Temperance and suffrage were closely linked by aspiration and opposition, nationally and in Nevada. Many women were involved in both activities, and the names of women involved in suffrage, discussed in the following chapter, are found in the records of several groups working for both campaigns. A resolution supporting suffrage, sent to Governor Boyle in 1920, illustrates the connections.

Mary Stanley Palmer was one of the women who signed the resolution. In 1889, when she was thirty years old, Palmer moved to Reno from her home in Waterville, Maine. Her husband had died the year before. At the urging of her father and an older sister, who were living in Reno, Palmer sold her home and furnishings and came

Let No Man Seek His Own, but Each His Neighbor's Good—1 Cor. 10:24, Rev. Ver.

Nevada
Woman's Christian Temperance Union

Sparks, Nevada, _____, 191__

RESOLUTION

Whereas: The need for early ratification of the Federal
Suffrage Amendment is every day increasingly apparent that
the women in such states as hold their Primaries in March
may have a voice in the choice of candidates,
        And because only two western suffrage states, of
which Nevada is one, have withheld ratification of the
Federal Suffrage Amendment;

Be it Resolved, that the State W.C.T.U. of Nevada and its
friends, do hereby petition Governor Emmet D. Boyle, Governor
of Nevada, to call a Special Session of the Legislature for
an early action on the Federal Suffrage Amendment.

Respectfully submitted:

Mrs. Maude C. Edwards, President
Mrs. Stella F. Snyder, Secretary
Mrs. J. S. McDonald
Mrs. B. M. Jones
Mrs. E. W. Van Deventer
Mrs. A. A. Off...
Mrs. T. St. Hazlett
Mrs. I. I. Nail
Miss Dora Stanley
Mary S. Palmer
Dora C. Prouty
Miss Nellie Whitney
Mrs. Mary C. Franzman

Another example of shared interests is this 1920 resolution from the Nevada WCTU in support of the federal suffrage amendment. (Nevada State Library & Archives)

Many of the women in this photograph, probably a women's church group circa 1917, signed the WCTU resolution sent to Governor Boyle. Sitting, left to right: Mrs. Jacobsen, Mary Palmer, Ethel Palmer, Lulla Murphy, Dora Stanley. Standing, left to right: Mrs. Lowther, Lucy Van Deventer, Mrs. Manson, Isabelle Ward, Minnie Black, Dora Prouty, Emma Palmer, Mrs. Olin Ward, Mrs. Romanzo Adams, Mary C. Franzman, Hattie Palmer. Names were recorded on the back of the photograph and many of the women's first names were not noted. (Special Collections, University of Nevada, Reno Library)

across country on the train with her three young sons. She used the money from her husband's estate to support herself in Reno for the next fifty-five years by loaning money. She lived on the interest charged, generally four percent, and helped put her children through college and graduate school.

The close connections in Reno around the turn of the century are clear in Palmer's physical location, as well as in her social activities. A picture taken in her front yard around 1917 was probably a gathering of a Methodist women's association. Many of the women in the photograph, also members of the Nevada WCTU, had signed the resolution to Governor Boyle. Several of them lived within a few blocks of Mary Palmer's home at the corner of Mill and Lake streets. Anne Martin, who was not in the photograph, but who was a leader of the suffrage movement in Nevada, had lived across the street. The interests and activities, and sometimes the physical proximity, of Nevada women operating in the public sphere were closely intertwined.

In 1914 women were victorious in one of their battles for expanded rights when Nevada joined several other western states and passed a constitutional amendment that allowed women to vote. Women with common interests were jubilant in their success. One women who had worked for suffrage, however, was disillusioned by the celebration of victory.

Mrs. R. Ronan expressed her disappointment in a letter to the editor of the *Elko Free Press* in November, 1914. Mrs. Ronan told the *Press*: "I have at all times stood strongly in favor of equal franchise, and even went to the length of standing in the street for three hours on election day begging every man that passed to vote in favor of the amendment and received the most courteous treatment." She explained that she was not asking for the vote as a gift. It was instead a "task and responsibility" that women would undertake out of concern for moral issues involved. She then received an invitation to a celebration to honor the victory on election day.

Mrs. Ronan enjoyed the speeches, but she was shocked at the conclusion of the party:

> Then, oh, the shame of it! two waitresses appeared upon the scene bearing trays with glasses filled with what might be supposed to be grape juice, but what proved to be something a great deal stronger, the flavor of which would indicate it had been mixed in the barroom . . . .In the opinion of this writer if this is the ideal toward

MRS. RONAN DEFINES SUFFRAGISTS' ATTITUDE

To the Free Press:

On last Saturday afternoon the undersigned had received a special invitation to attend a celebration given in honor of the victory of the women on election day which granted them equal franchise with the men. I believe in credit where credit is due and the talk given by the English suffrage worker in defense of her militant sisters was interesting and instructive.

I have at all times stood strongly in favor of equal franchise, and even went to the length of standing in the street for three hours on election day begging every man that passed to vote in favor of the amendment and received the most courteous treatment. But I want everyone to know that I was not asking these men to give the ballot to Nevada women as a present, an ornament, a toy or a treat, but as a task and responsibility, for not in rights but in duties should women's interest be based in the modern movement which is founded chiefly in her concern in the moral issues involved. This new opportunity enforces the duty to embody in her own civic life and in the body politic much needed moral vigor and highest motives. After the talk at the meeting and several of the women present had expressed their satisfaction at the result of the election, a resolution of thanks was voted the men of Nevada. Then, oh, the shame of it! two waitresses appeared upon the scene bearing trays with glasses filled with what might be supposed to be grape juice, but what proved to be something a great deal stronger, the flavor of which would indicate it had been mixed in the barroom. I tasted the liquor and felt an impulse to shatter the glass on the floor, but for politeness sake I simply placed the glass and its contents on the table. And again to the shame of the womanhood of Nevada it seems this one celebration was not enough, but a large card party to take place soon was announced and committees appointed to arrange for it.

In the opinion of the writer if this is the ideal toward which the Nevada women are going to use their liberty I want to say here and now that I am heartily sorry that I have helped in any way to bring to them the responsibility to which I had been accustomed in my native state, and which I am proud to say has been used to the honor and credit of womanhood, and if the giving of card parties and serving spiritous drinks for celebration is the way of expressing the Nevada woman's ideal of the larger liberty, then surely the "anti's" had strongest grounds for their arguments, for they evidently knew the Nevada women better than I. But in justice to many of the women who were present it is only right to say that they were not given an opportunity at the meeting to express themselves in regard to the card party celebration.

MRS. R. RONAN

SPARKS WONAN NEW PRESIDENT

Thirteenth Annual Convention Of W. C. T. U. Meets In Reno

The 30th annual convention of the Nevada W. C. T. U. was held in the Baptist church in West Second street yesterday morning, afternoon and evening. Delegates from all sections of the state were in attendance. The meeting was called to order at 10 o'clock in the morning and following the appointment of various committees reports of the offices were read.

Progress was the keynote of all of the officers' reports. Memorial services were conducted by Mrs. Van Deventer. Mrs. F. G. Patrick addressed the delegates during the afternoon, presenting greetings from the General Federation of Women's Clubs. The address of the president, Mrs. Linville, was read during the afternoon session. Mrs. Helen D. Harford also spoke during the afternoon.

A short session was held during the evening, comprising a song and praise service and an address by Mrs. Harford.

The following officers were elected to serve for the next 12 months: Mrs. F. R. Linville, of Sparks, President; Mrs. F. H. Church, vice-president; Mrs. F. G. Emon, recording secretary; Mrs. Maud Edwards, of Sparks, corresponding secretary; Mrs. O. M. Wel-

Right Reno Evening Gazette, *October 10, 1914*
Temperance activities and meetings were reported in the newspapers. The names listed in the articles can provide useful pieces of the historical puzzle of Nevada women and their lives. (Nevada State Library & Archives)

Left Elko Free Press, *November 9, 1914*
Women were often involved in a number of reform causes. Mrs. R. Ronan worked for suffrage and also supported temperance. She was offended when she found that the grape juice at the victory celebration was fermented, and tasted, as she characterized it, like something "that had been mixed in the barroom." (Nevada State Library & Archives)

which the Nevada women are going to use their liberty I want to say here and now that I am heartily sorry that I have helped in any way. . .

Offended by the dishonorable actions of the newly enfranchised, Mrs. Ronan concluded that the "antis" must have understood better the character of Nevada women, who were apparently too weak to resist the temptation of strong drink.

As evident from this incident, women did have access to and did consume alcohol. As well as partaking of alcoholic beverages that might be kept in the home, many women relied upon tonics and remedies commonly taken for a variety of ailments, from tooth ache to "female troubles," which generally had a high alcohol content. And recent archeological investigation and findings in Virginia City indicate that saloons were not necessarily the sole domain of men and "women of bad repute." Several of the sites of bars from the heyday of the Comstock Lode are providing evidence that entire families, men, women and children, frequented saloons, making them, as State Historic Preservation Officer Ron James has phrased it, "something like the nineteenth-century version of the pizza parlor." Whether this custom was unique to Virginia City, to certain bars in Virginia City, or limited in both scale and time frame is not clear. Archeological investigation continues, providing important sources of information about the lives of women from Nevada's past.

Despite occasional disappointment in the behavior of their comrades in the battle against strong drink, women persevered in their crusade. Temperance organizations printed and distributed rosters listing the dry legislative candidates, one of whom was the first female legislator, Sadie Hurst, for the 1918 election. Still, on a local level, associations like the Nevada WCTU and the Anti-Saloon League could not overcome the political and economic power of supporters of alcohol consumption, dubbed "the saloon crowd." Saloons were often the center of social life for men, especially in small towns and mining centers.

In one locale, help came from an unexpected source. In the copper mining areas of eastern Nevada, company towns were established to house mine workers and supervisory personnel. The companies controlled virtually every aspect of life in the company towns, including what businesses operated within city limits. Saloons, later known as pool halls, were strictly controlled and limited in company

DRY LEGISLATIVE CANDIDATES

SENATORS

VOTE FOR ONE

M. P. MACMILLAN, Democrat.
R. H. COWLES, Republican.

ASSEMBLYMEN

VOTE FOR FIVE

JOSEPH F. McDONALD, Democrat.
GEORGE ARMSTRONG, Democrat.
ARTHUR F. LASHER, Republican.
ERNEST MACK, Republican.
MRS. SADIE HURST, Republican.
H. E. STEWART, Republican.
JOHN S. SINAI, Republican.

ANTI-SALOON LEAGUE

Temperance groups provided voters with the names of those candidates who supported the dry cause. (Nevada Historical Society)

If Either Prohibition Amendment is Adopted

No Hotel, Cafe or Restaurant could serve wine or liquor, not even with meals.

No social or Fraternal Organization or Club could offer wine or liquor to guests or members.

No grocery or family liquor store could sell wine or liquor in sealed packages.

No summer resort could serve or give away wines or liquor to visitors or guests.

No wine or liquor could be served at picnics or gatherings in any park or public place.

No tourist visiting the State could purchase wine or other liquor.

VOTE "NO" ON BOTH AMENDMENTS
1 and 2, NOVEMBER 7, 1916

UNITED CALIFORNIA INDUSTRIES
310 HUMBOLDT BANK BUILDING
SAN FRANCISCO

150

Ballot Titles of Prohibition Amendments on Ballot November 7, 1916

VOTE "NO" ON BOTH AMENDMENTS

1 "PROHIBITION. Initiative measure adding Article XXIV to Constitution. Defines alcoholic liquor. After January 1, 1920, prohibits the manufacture, sale or possession of same, except for medicinal, sacramental, scientific and mechanical purposes under restrictions prescribed by law. Prescribes and authorizes penalties. Declares payment of Internal Revenue Tax prima facie evidence of violation. Declares this amendment shall not affect prohibitory liquor laws, or ordinances, enacted before such date, or be construed as in conflict with Article XXIV-A of Constitution if latter article is adopted, and that this amendment supersedes that article on that date."

Yes	.
No	X

Stamp "X" Here

2 "INITIATIVE AMENDMENT, ADDING ARTICLE XXIV-A TO CONSTITUTION. Defines alcoholic liquor; after January 1, 1918, prohibits its possession, gift or sale in saloon, dram shop, dive, store, hotel, restaurant, club, dance hall or other place of public resort; prohibits sale, accepting or soliciting orders anywhere, except in pharmacies for certain purposes and by manufacturers on premises where manufactured, under delivery and quantity restrictions. Owner or manager of all such places to prevent drinking therein. Restricts transportation. Payment Internal Revenue Tax prima facie evidence of violation. Prescribes and authorizes penalties. Neither repeals nor limits state or local prohibition, or Article XXIV of Constitution."

Yes	
No	X

Stamp "X" Here

150

(Over)

Not everyone championed the cause of temperance. Many businesses would suffer economically with a Prohibition amendment, and they lobbied publicly against changes in the laws. (Nevada Historical Society)

towns like McGill in White Pine county. In his memoirs of his boyhood in White Pine County, *Growing Up in a Company Town*, Russell Elliott recalled there were only two saloons in McGill while the company operated the community. Despite the money that the mining companies could generate in their company owned businesses, including saloons, a sober labor force was more productive. It was generally considered prudent to limit access to alcoholic beverages.

Ultimately the victory over strong drink, albeit temporary, came on the national level. By 1917, liquor had been outlawed in nineteen states. The WCTU and Anti-Saloon Leagues on both a national and local level had been largely responsible for these gains. Nevada squeaked in before national Prohibition in November, 1918, when the manufacture and sale of all intoxicating beverages was prohibited in the state. It was the first use of the initiative process since its creation by constitutional amendment in 1912.

On the federal level it was the First World War that provided the final impetus for success. Supporters of prohibition portrayed a dry nation as a patriotic nation. Suspect German-owned breweries would be forced out of business, and nutritious grains used in the manufacture of alcoholic beverages would be available for the fighting men of America. The Eighteenth Amendment, which made the manufacture, transport, or sale of alcoholic beverages illegal, passed in Congress in December 1917. It was hailed as a progressive and public-spirited move for the good of the nation. The amendment was ratified in 1919. Nevada was the forty-first state to ratify. The Eighteenth Amendment, Prohibition, went into effect in January 1920. The entire nation went dry, or nearly so.

Temperance supporters were jubilant. The Nevada WCTU hosted a victory banquet at the Baptist Church in Reno. They invited Governor and Mrs. Boyle to the celebration. The governor was instructed to prepare a three-minute speech on "Victory In War," to coincide with the other planned speeches on Victory in Suffrage and Victory in Prohibition.

The work of the reformers was not done, however. In 1919, prompted by the WCTU, the legislature passed AB98 which created Frances Willard Day. It was celebrated on September 28, the anniversary of her birth in 1839. The bill required teachers to devote a portion of the day to temperance education. It was repealed in 1956.

Nationwide Prohibition was a rather spectacular failure. The

LET NO MAN SEEK HIS OWN, BUT EACH HIS NEIGBBOR'S GOOD—1 COR. 10:24, REV. VER.

Nevada Woman's Christian Temperance Union

Sparks Nev.
Oct. 22–1919

To The Hon. Governor Emmet D. Boyle
Carson Nev.

Dear Governor Boyle:—
The Annual Convention of The Woman's Christian Temperance Union Of Nevada will be held in Reno, Nov. 3–4, in the Baptist Church; and we shall be pleased if you and Mrs. Boyle can arrange to be wit at a "Victory Banquet," on Monday evening Nov. 3 at Seven o'clock, in the church dining room

Three minute speeches will be given, on "Victories—In War, In Suffrage and In Prohibit

The topic

Hoping we

presence,

Let No Man Seek His Own but Each His Neighbor's Good—
1 Cor. 10:24, Rev. Ver.

Woman's Christian Temperance Union of Nevada

Time of Prayer—Noontide
Badge—A Knot of White Ribbon
Watchwords—Agitate, Educate Organize

Reno, Nevada, ...Oct. 17............192 1

His Excellency,

Governor Emmet D. Boyle,

Carson City, Nev.

My dear Governor:—

The State Convention of the Woman's Christian Temperance Union is to be held in Reno, Nevada, Oct. 25-26 at the Baptist Church.

We are to hold an Americanization evening on Oct. 25th and it is the pleasure of the Union that you address the convention at this time, if it does not interfere with your other duties.

Trusting that you will see your way clear to do this, we are,

Very Respectfully,

WOMAN'S CHRISTIAN TEMPERANCE UNION.

By *Fannie J Miller*

State Corresponding Sec'y.

446 S. Virginia St.,
Reno, Nev.

This Nevada WCTU letterhead provides a wealth of information. WCTU departments are listed, along with superintendent names, and indicates the variety of issues that members of the WCTU addressed. (Nevada State Library & Archives)

Governor Emmet Boyle supported many reform issues. The Nevada WCTU invited him to speak at their victory banquet celebrating the success of prohibition in 1919. (Nevada State Library & Archives)

Volstead Act created a Prohibition Bureau within the Treasury Department, but the agency was underfunded and generally ineffective. Speakeasies abounded in Nevada and throughout the nation. Nevada had passed its own liquor prohibition before the national amendment, but Russell Elliott noted the development of a solid "wet" sentiment. By 1926 there were two antiprohibition measures on the ballot. One was a petition to call a constitutional convention to repeal prohibition. The other presented voters with an opportunity to endorse a legislative resolution opposing constitutional prohibition. Nevada voters approved both measures.

The political climate did not favor Prohibition. A 1934 *Fortune* article about Reno, "Passion in the Desert," discussed Reno Mayor E. E. Roberts. The magazine asserted that Roberts, mayor of Reno throughout most of the 1920s, had announced from the pulpit of the Methodist church that his solution for bootlegging was that "brimming barrels of whiskey should stand on every street corner in Reno." Against such public sentiments from elected officials, temperance organizations faced an uphill, and ultimately unsuccessful battle. The Eighteenth Amendment was repealed in 1933.

The Nevada WCTU did not halt its attempts to purify and improve Nevada society, however. Local unions throughout the state continued to file annual reports. The Smith Valley union reported in 1941 that they had eleven paid members, the same as the year before. The report also noted the difficulty of meeting regularly, "as those interested carry heavy work in other organizations." Smith Valley members had contributed $2.00 each to the legislative fund and to the Willard Memorial Fund. Records from the Nevada WCTU indicate activity well into the 1980s.

The temperance movement in Nevada and nationally was closely connected to other women's organizations and activities. Suffrage groups were among those organizations intimately entwined with the membership and the ultimate goals of temperance. As with temperance, suffrage activity in Nevada was another early social and political venue for Nevada women emerging into public life. It was also a significant forum through which Nevada women demonstrated the truth of the statement, "They cannot be *a* people without us." The "people" could only become a meaningful concept when basic political rights were granted to half of the population.

Anne Martin and supporters took to the dirty, dusty, and rocky roads of backcountry Nevada to convince voters to support suffrage. (University of Nevada, Reno, Special Collections)

> WHATEVER we may think of woman's right to vote and legislate, there can be no disputing her right to bare arms, and the prettier the better and more irresistible. This is a right descended from Mother Eve.

Gold Hill Daily News, *December 26, 1867*
The issue of women voting often suffered insidious attacks of bad jokes.
(Nevada State Library & Archives)

WOMEN AND THE VOTE IN NEVADA

In her memoirs of the suffrage campaign, published in the *University of Nevada Bulletin* in August, 1948, Anne Martin recalled the work of a "small group of voteless women, working for three years almost night and day," who managed to convince "reluctant male voters" that women were also entitled to voting rights. There was indeed a flurry of activity between 1912 and 1914, but the effort to bring women into the electorate began much earlier and encompassed decades rather than years. The suffrage battle was fought throughout the state, led by local women bringing a variety of experience and tactics to the movement. But Nevada's hard fought crusade was part of the larger campaign, skirmishes fought by determined and politically savvy women throughout the western region and the nation.

Initially, public debate in Nevada over suffrage for women centered on the Comstock. As early as 1867 Laura de Force Gordon was lecturing to audiences in Virginia City and Gold Hill. Gordon was well known for her work as a spiritualist. Public appearances by those who claimed to communicate with those who had "passed over" were popular events that drew large crowds in Nevada as well as throughout the nation. Gordon was a noted speaking medium who went beyond the supernatural in her lectures, and included a justification for women's rights with her spiritual presentation. After a trip to California, Gordon returned to Virginia City again the following year. She then went further afield to Austin, in the center of the state, to carry her message that the right to vote should be based on education, not gender or race.

Gordon was a powerful and persuasive voice for her cause, but it wasn't only women who were supportive of women's right to the vote. A Storey County representative to the legislature, Curtis J. Hillyer, backed the movement and introduced an amendment to the Nevada constitution in 1869 to have the word "male" removed from the suf-

NEW TO-DAY.

BALLOT FOR WOMAN!

LECTURE

—BY—

LAURA DeFORCE GORDON

—AT—

PIPER'S OPERA HOUSE,

THIS (FRIDAY) EVENING.

—

SUBJECT:

WOMAN'S ENFRANCHISEMENT.

ADMISSION • • • • • • • • $1 00

Lecture to commence at 8 o'clock.   jy22 1t

Territorial Enterprise, *July 22, 1870*
*Laura deForce Gordon was a staunch
and active supporter of women's
suffrage. (Nevada State Library &
Archives)*

Carson Daily Appeal, *February 14,
1869*
*Women's suffrage was discussed
seriously by some editors despite the
patronizing tone that marked some of
the newspaper debate over the issue of
women and the vote. (Nevada State
Library & Archives)*

perform the functions of the [...] Examiners; who would make splendid and attractive Speakers of the Assembly; who would be graceful and useful Senators; who would add beauty and purity to the Judiciary; who would, perhaps, make reliable State Printers—but we are a little in doubt upon this last proposition; and everybody is acquainted with "any quantity" of ladies who would run the primaries upon an improved plan and make the polls a much more agreeable arrangement than they are at present. Let the ladies vote and you fortify and purify politics as they cannot, by other means be so improved.

In all seriousness, we believe in giving the right to vote to women. They are as much a part of the responsible people as their fathers and brothers and husbands; and as to their influence upon politics, we all know, that even without the vote, they exercise a control over those with whom they are brought in contact which is of a very strong and decisive character. The law compels them to pay taxes and it should, in deference to the true spirit of republicanism, accord them the right to a voice in the selection of those who are to make and administer the laws that are to govern their actions and affect their property. The Constitution as it now stands virtually says that woman is inferior to man in an intellectual point of view. There is but a poor showing of "Mother wit" in that tacit declaration. It may be possible that not so many as one half the women of this State desire to be vested with the right to vote and hold office; but we contend that if there be no more than one woman who, feeling the responsibilities and immunities of a citizen and tax payer, asks to have the power given into her hands for the purpose of exercising that self protection without which the citizen is measurably powerless in relation to those who have a voice in the administration of the Government, she should have it; and that until she and all others of her sex who feel as she does are so placed upon an equality with other citizens of the commonwealth, "a republican form of Government" as contemplated by the Declaration of American Independence is disregarded and set at naught. The rule ought to be established that every citizen of every degree should be, in reality, as he and she are, by law contemplated to be, a full and equal participant in the Government which "derives its just powers from the consent of the governed."

frage clause. That tiny alteration would have had huge consequences. There was no national law preventing women from voting; restrictions on the franchise were determined on a state level. Both houses approved the measure, and as required to amend the state constitution, the bill was sent to the Secretary of State to be introduced again in the next biennial session in 1871.

The issue of the *Carson Daily Appeal* for February 14, 1869 supported women's suffrage when an editorial posed the question, "What sort of equality is it which thus makes 'male whites of adult age' the sole and exclusive participants in the exercise of the elective franchise?" It wasn't until the following year, 1870, that the Fifteenth Amendment to the U. S. Constitution granted voting rights to African-American males. The omission of the franchise for women angered and disappointed many women who had worked hard for abolition of slavery, and the granting of civil rights to enslaved people of both genders.

Although Nevada legislators and some newspaper editors viewed suffrage favorably, there was significant opposition to voting women, and much of it was expressed publicly. Not all of the objections came from men. In a letter to the *Territorial Enterprise* in Virginia City, Mrs. Anna Fitch, wife of Congressman Thomas Fitch, clearly articulated the opinions of many men and women regarding the appropriate place for women—and, in Fitch's view, a woman's place was not standing next to a ballot box fulfilling her civic responsibility. Fitch eloquently and passionately argued that women, "whole women," were happiest and most effective when performing their natural emotional and nurturing duties within the home.

In July of that year the *Elko Independent* expressed criticism of another newspaper in the state, the *Humboldt Register* in Winnemucca, for its inability to stand firm on a suffrage position. They reprinted the *Register's* editorial, which asserted that the newspaper had been mistakenly identified as "a dauntless champion and defender of the down-trodden and defenseless of our race." The *Register* referred to the expected victory for women as the time when "females will be females no longer." Criticism for women with civic aspirations came from other sources as well. Several months previously the *Register* had printed a comment regarding women and voting from Lander County that referred to a genuine school marm as "one who does not aspire to the exalted privilege of voting—one, who, if she has not,

Mrs. Anna Fitch's attack on women voting used many of the social ideals in vogue regarding women and the domestic sphere. (Photograph, Nevada Historical Society)

course—are to be found mainly in her impulses. This would be a strong point: if it did not prove too much. But woman's nature is wholly emotional; she does nothing worth the doing except through the channel of the sympathies.

"The world of the affections is her world,
Not that of man's ambition."

She idealizes, and sublimates, and, in a word, deifies somebody; that is, if she is a whole woman. The object may be ever so vicious, ever so unworthy, but if he is equal to her love he is equal to her faith, and she reposes naturally enough in his judgment. Now how many of these, do you imagine, would deliberately vote in

Territorial Enterprise, *April 25, 1869*

will follow the noble example of a true woman and have the boys vote for her."

There was also, however, public support for women's voting rights. The next year, in 1870, a Humboldt County legislator, Senator M. S. Bonnifield, backed the suffrage movement when he proposed a statewide suffrage convention. A small group of supporters gathered in Battle Mountain on July 4, "for the purpose of effecting an organization." Laura de Force Gordon was elected president and embarked on a speaking tour around the state, with mixed success. The *Elko Independent* described her address as "the most powerful address we have ever heard fall from the lips of a woman. . ." Not all were as impressed. In contrast, the *Reno Crescent* reported, "from all that we had read and heard of the lady we had formed a very exalted opinion of her forensic and argumentative abilities, and as a consequence suffered a serious disappointment."

The issue of women's voting rights was not a new topic of social and political debate in the United States. The maelstrom of reform activity in antebellum America provided fertile ground in which to cultivate demands for equality. Efforts to right a variety of social wrongs, especially slavery, highlighted the discrepancies in the social and legal position of women. Early organization of a women's movement had started with the Women's Rights Convention at Seneca Falls, New York in 1848. The Declaration of Rights and Sentiments signed there encompassed much more than voting rights. The women supporting the convention ideals were interested in correcting inequities regarding property, education, divorce, employment and wages, among others. In fact, voting rights were considered radical, and some delegates hesitated about inclusion of this demand. Of the twelve resolutions passed at the convention, the call for women's suffrage was the only one that did not pass unanimously.

The struggle to attain women's rights was closely connected to efforts to attain racial equality. With the end of conflict between the states, feminists like Lucy Stone, Elizabeth Cady Stanton and Susan B. Anthony expected that women, along with African-American men, would receive voting rights. Many were angry and bitter when the Fourteenth and Fifteenth Amendments to the U. S. Constitution mandated political rights for former male slaves, but ignored the issue of women's rights.

The failure to gain recognition for their sex generated a shift in

POLITICALLY

We do care whether school keeps or not. We want school to keep, and more, we want it kept by a genuine "school marm," one who does not aspire to the exalted privilege of voting—one who, if she has not, will follow the noble example of a true woman and have boys to vote for her. Moreover our good wife does not wish the right of franchise, from which fact we infer that "nine-tenths" of the women here are not "on it."   LANDER.

Humboldt Register, *June 4, 1870*
Newspapers attacked each other regarding the women's right to vote. (Nevada State Library & Archives)

R   m18tf

WOMAN SUFFRAGE

Convention!

AS THE last Legislature has proposed an Amendment to the State Constitution by which women may be enfranchised, therefore, in order that the issue may be fairly brought before the electors of this State at the ensuing election, the friends of the measure in Humboldt county are requested to meet in Mass Convention, at BATTLE MOUNTAIN, on

Monday, 4th Day of July, 1870,

for the purpose of effecting an organization. The friends of Female Suffrage throughout the State are respectfully invited to be present for consultation and to devise the best means of perfecting a State organization. The following distinguished advocates of the cause have been invited to address the convention:

Mrs. J. N. Huie, of Winnemucca; Miss Anna M. Dodge, of Chicago; Theodore Tilton; Gov. Safford, of Arizona; Miss Gordon Bennett; C. J. Hillyer, of Nevada; S. F. Lewis, of Reno Crescent; Gov. J. A. Campbell, of Wyoming.

GEO. W. FOX,   T. V. JULIEN,
C. F. GOODING,   M. S. BONNIFIELD,
        DAVID MELARKIE.
        Committee of Arrangements.
April 16, 1870   25-tf

Humboldt Register, *July 2, 1870*
The Woman Suffrage Convention was held in Battle Mountain, Nevada in July, 1870. (Nevada State Library & Archives)

direction for many women, and resulted in a split among advocates for women's rights. Two separate groups, the National Woman Suffrage Association (1869) and the American Woman Suffrage Association (1870) were formed. The National group, led by Stanton and Anthony, envisioned the franchise for women as a tool to gain other social and economic rights. Stone headed the American group, which focused on a single issue, that of women's voting rights. The two organizations worked independently until they merged in 1890.

Nationally, the suffrage movement earned the enmity of the liquor lobby, and was damaged by its association with the Temperance movement. Frances Willard, long time leader of the Women's Christian Temperance Union, campaigned for women's voting rights in order to use the vote to further temperance goals. After Willard's death in 1898 the WCTU abandoned the suffrage cause, but the association remained in the minds of many voting men who feared voting women would put the saloons out of business.

The western states proved to be more politically receptive than those in the east to the idea of votes for women. Wyoming Territory enfranchised women in 1869. Nevada came close to duplicating that liberal legislation when the suffrage amendment was considered a second time, in 1871. Laura de Force Gordon urged passage in a speech before the Assembly. Unfortunately Curtis Hillyer, the assemblyman who had introduced the amendment in the previous legislature, and other suffrage backers did not return to the legislature, and without strong support the amendment was narrowly defeated.

Some public opinion was openly critical of the failure of the legislature to act for the political rights of women. On February 18, 1871, the *Nevada State Journal* lamented the fate of women in Nevada who were obliged "by a barbarous and tyrannical Legislature to continue suffering." In its assessment the newspaper reached the conclusion that the "Assembly is not overstocked with brains."

The loss of that particular effort to obtain the vote was by no means the obituary for the suffrage movement in Nevada. Leaders from national suffrage associations toured the country, working to encourage local organization and to break down resistance to woman franchise. Their tours included trips to the west and to Nevada. In August, 1871, Elizabeth Cady Stanton spoke in Virginia City and Carson City. One newspaper account deemed it a "very sound and sensible lecture," and noted that one hundred and twenty-five ladies

WHY WOMEN SHOULD VOTE

Views of Two Little Girls of the East Fork District School

By Lillie Jacobsen, Age 14.

Women should vote because they have to work just as men do and some times they have to work for lower wages than men.

Women who have land have to pay taxes on it, so they should help say how the money should be used.

Women must obey the laws just as men do and if they don't obey them they are punished.

If women should not vote they ought not have to obey the laws or pay taxes.

Women have to suffer from bad government just as men have to. If they shouldn't vote they ought not to suffer from bad government.

The constitution says that the government is of the people, by the people and for the people. And the women are people.

Some people say that the women should pay poll taxes too if they want to vote. I guess if they want to vote they will pay poll taxes.

Some people say that women are supposed to fight if they vote. And the people say that women are afraid to fight and they don't know how to shoot. But if you read in the newspapers, it says that some women can shoot even better than men.

Not all the men that are living today have have fought in battles.

Another thing: a mother wants to make a better family of her children which the men never take interest in. And that is another reason why they should vote.

And there are many other reasons why women should vote.

By Alma Settelmeyer, Age 15.

The women need the vote because they are people just the same as the men.

The men think the women should stay home and mind her business, while they go and make the laws.

The women have to care for the children's health and if they get canned fruit and vegetables, etc. at the store and the fruit is spoiled, she feeds it to the children and they get sick, whose fault is it? It's the men's fault because they have to care for the food.

The woman is responsible for the cleanliness of her house. The man isn't.

She is responsible if the children are not brought up right.

The women can hold office just as well as the men.

Women have to work for lower wages than men in some cases.

Women have to pay tax on the land they own even if they do not vote. So why can't they vote? They should not pay tax because they do not vote.

If they do not obey the laws they get punished for it, when they ought not because they have no right to help make the laws.

Men think the women cannot stand a long strain, but some women have to raise a large family and stand around a hot stove and do the cooking for the family and a large bunch of men besides.

Men may think that everything will go wrong when the women begin to vote, but they better wait till the women vote in Nevada and then talk.

Record Courier, April 24, 1914 School girls used arguments similar to those debated by state and national women leaders. (Nevada State Library & Archives)

Mary S. Doten (wife of Alf Doten, Comstock journalist and diarist) stated her views on the vote. Mary Doten was a teacher and school administrator in Washoe County. (Nevada Historical Society)

attended. Susan B. Anthony also came to Nevada later that year, lecturing in Carson City and Virginia City.

Additional attempts were made to introduce and pass suffrage amendments throughout the 1870s and 1880s. An 1883 bill passed in the Senate but did not make it through the Assembly. In 1887, the Senate and Assembly passed separate measures but could not come to a workable compromise. In the next biennial session another suffrage measure lost in the Assembly.

By 1890 a newly merged National American Woman Suffrage Association, headed by Elizabeth Cady Stanton, emerged with hopes to reinvigorate the national cause. There was still disagreement on the national level. Some feminists, Susan B. Anthony among them, believed that success would be achieved with the passage of an amendment to the national constitution. Others, especially women representing southern and western states, advocated campaigns to gain the vote though state legislation.

Mary Stoddard Doten was one of the women involved in a variety of public activities. She was married to Alf Doten, and much of what is known about her life is recorded in the journals that her husband kept until his death in 1903. Doten failed to provide adequate support for his family, and Mary Doten returned to a teaching career in Reno in 1884. She was also a journalist and poet, and expressed her resentment over the lack of equality for women. Angered at having women linked with "idiots, lunatics, and paupers," Doten published a poem in 1890, and predicted that men would eventually join those ranks themselves, "Far, far below good woman!"

The fight for the vote, of course, went beyond expressions of opinion through poetry. Women in Nevada continued to target the state legislature in the 1890s. The Lucy Stone Nonpartisan Equal Suffrage League was organized in Austin in 1894. Frances Williamson, who was a leader in that association, contributed a great deal to the suffrage cause in Nevada. A native of Canada, Williamson emigrated to Austin in 1863 to teach. Within two years she was principal, and the following year she married John Williamson. Her new husband was superintendent of schools, owned a mercantile business, and later became a state Senator from Lander county.

The Williamsons settled in to married life and had six children. In the mid-1870s, four of their children died. When their fifth child, a son who was living in Carson City, died in 1891, John Williamson

Anna Shaw was one of several prominent national leaders who traveled to Nevada, and other western states, to speak for women's suffrage. (Nevada Historical Society)

You are cordially invited
to meet

Dr. Anna Howard Shaw

at the home of
Mrs. W. O'H. Martin,
157 Mill Street,
Monday October fifth
three to five.

Reception Committee:

Mrs. F. O. Norton   *Mrs. Geo. H. Taylor*
Mrs. Frances G. Newlands   *Mrs. William O'H. Martin*
Mrs. Samuel Belford   *Mrs. Prince A. Hawkins*

The Nevada Citizen.

A Journal Devoted to the Best Interests of Our Commonwealth.

VOL. I.   RENO, NEVADA, JUNE, 1897.   No. 4.

GROWTH OF THE AMERICAN NATION.

[Continued From Last Issue.]

THE Constitution of the United States is different from any other known or described by political philosophers. It belongs to the Grac-Roman family and is a republic, as distinguished from despotic constitutions, but it comes under the head of neither monarchy nor aristocracy, neither democratic nor mixed, but purely the product of American genius, for the realization of great ideas according to the divine plan, because it seeks to attain the end of wise and just government, by means unknown to the ancients. The American States are all sovereign States united, but disunited, are no States at all. In the formation of the Union the States were the creator, the Union the object created. Hence America is the name of our country, the United States is the name expressive of our political organization.

When the Constitution was sent to the Congress of Confederation, that body referred it to the legislatures of the several States for ratification. At first it met with vigorous opposition from men whose integrity and patriotism were above reproach. They were influenced by the historic fact that all national misery and retrogression is the result of the abuse of power, hence they hesitated to trust general government with the power conferred upon it by the Constitution. They entertained the idea that the safeguards of liberty were centered in State sovereignty. This would be impossible, because the Constitution says nothing about the formation of a compact with sovereign States. The people speak throughout the document and they speak with the voice of authority vested in American citizenship. They positively state what power the government shall exercise, and what powers it shall not exercise. It is self-evident that our government is inherent in and founded upon the will of the people of the States in their united capacity, not in their sovereign capacity.

Still, the advanced thinkers and statesmen of that day feared that in the office of President of the United States was disguised all the power vested in kings. This alone would have prevented the adoption of the Constitution, had it not been taken for granted that Washington would be the first President. The people firmly believed that the reins of government and the destiny of the new born nation would be safe in the keeping of him who had led them to one of greatest victories ever achieved in the struggle for human rights. The social and civic standing of Washington controlled more influence in favor of the adoption of the Constitution than the arguments in favor of its provisions.

No man ever stood for so much to his countrymen and to mankind as did Washington. It is conceded by commentators that he scored two of the greatest points in politics and diplomacy it is permitted man to attempt. "He maintained by peace the independence of his country which he conquered by war." "He founded a free government in the name of the principles of order and established their sway." Lord Brougham, the scholar of England, said: "Until time shall be no more, will a test of the progress which our race has made in wisdom and virtue be derived from the veneration paid to the immortal name of Washington." Fox, the greatest parliamentary orator who ever swayed the British House of Commons, said: "Illustrious man, before whom all borrowed greatness sinks into insignificance."

Foremost among those who employed their pens in explaining and defending the Constitution, were James Madison, Alexander Hamilton and John Jay. Their articles published under the title of "Federalist" were conceded to be the ablest interpretations (of the Constitution) because they satisfactorily explained why they found it expedient to reject all previous forms of written constitutions and frame one which should draw its vitality from the conscience of the people in their several capacity and in their united capacity. This was a new contribution to political science, and from the fact of its originality, it was but imperfectly understood by the average statesmen and citizens of that day, as it is in a sense by some statesmen and citizens of the present day, who too often seek to explain its wise provisions by analogy borrowed from older constitutions, rather than by a profound study of the peculiar merits of its principles. The tendency of American politics then, as now, was in the direction of centralization, and a disposition to exalt party above people, just as if American citizenship had for its mission only the reproduction of ancient Athens. This is an attempt to clothe the present and the future in the cast off garments of the past. Hence the work of the individual citizen and statesman of to-day is even more difficult than the victories won by brave armies of the past.

When the legislatures of the several States called conventions to consider the adoption of the Constitution, it brought together the brain power of both Federalists and anti-Federalists, and each sustained their convictions in regard to it by the most astute political philosophy recorded in the history of our civil government. The question under debate was: "Did the Constitution form a national government of the people, for the people of the United States, or was it to be regarded as a compact, or league between sovereign States?" The first view was the one entertained by the framers of the Constitution, and accepted by a majority of the people, while the second view was the one accepted by a minority who were advocates of State sovereignty, of whom John C. Calhoun was the acknowledged champion. He maintained that the States existed before the Union and were therefore sovereign, and if the States went into the convention of sovereign States, they came out sovereign States—hence his radical doctrine was, that sovereignty was vested in the States severally after the convention as before it. Calhoun himself was no secessionist, but he laid the premises from which secession is the logical conclusion. Although the Civil War vindicated the sovereignty vested in the Union when it defeated the armed forces of the seceding States, it has not eradicated the doctrine, for the spirit of State's rights crops out in the writings of some of our ablest political philosophers.

In the several conventions the bearing of those who were out-voted is worthy of notice. The most determined opponents, when the vote for adoption of Constitution was announced, without a single exception, pledged themselves to support it; since a majority had seen fit to adopt it, they would use their utmost endeavors to induce their constituents

Continued on Fourth Page.

The Nevada Citizen, "A Journal Devoted to the Best Interests of Our Commonwealth" (Nevada Historical Society)

History of the Suffrage Movement in Nevada
1900 — by 1913
By Jeanne Elizabeth Weir.

Since nineteen hundred nothing had been done to advance the
cause of Woman Suffrage in Nevada although a few laws had been
enacted for the benefit of women and children.

On November 1, 1909 Mrs. Mackay, president of the Equal Franchise
Society, wrote from New York to Miss Jeanne Elizabeth Wier asking
whether a local branch of the Society could not be started in
Nevada.[1] Because of double duties as head of the department of
history and political science in the University of Nevada and as
executive secretary of the Nevada Historical Society, Miss Wier
was loath to undertake another line of work. But when in New York
attending the annual meeting of the American Historical Association
at the next holiday season, she conferred with Mrs. Mackay relative
to the situation in Nevada and plans were made for the launching of
a branch organization in January, 1910.[2] However an illness of
several months' duration deferred the work until autumn. Then a
pledge to assist in the organization of an Equal Franchise Society
in Reno was circulated by Miss Wier and was signed by Dr. J. E.
Stubbs and Mrs. Stubbs, Miss Alice B. Armstrong, Librarian J. D.
Layman, Mrs. Geo. E. Taylor, Mrs. Margaret Stanislawsky, Dr. C. A.
Jacobson, Mrs. Julia F. Bender, Dr. and Mrs. J. E. Church, Miss
Laura de Laguna, Miss Kate Bardenwerper, Mrs. A. E. Hershiser,
Mrs. Alice A. Chism, Mrs. Page, Judge Hibbard and A. Grant Miller,
and later in the year by many others.

------------------ ---------   --- --- - - ------------------------

Reno Evening Gazette, Jan. 10, 1910.

Jeanne Weir was active in the suffrage campaign, and wrote a brief history to
record her memories of the historically significant events. (Nevada Historical
Society)

POSTAL TELEGRAPH – COMMERCIAL CABLES

CLARENCE H. MACKAY, PRESIDENT.

DELIVERY NO.

(104)

TELEGRAM

RECEIVED
RENO, NEV.

The Postal Telegraph-Cable Company (Incorporated) transmits and delivers this message subject to the terms and conditions printed on the back of this blank.

DESIGN PATENT APPLIED FOR.

12 SF Ls. 43.

New York January 28th 1911.

Miss Jeanne Elizabeth Weier,

Reno Nevada.

May Nevada do Justice to the Women of this Generation because of
these who made the Forty Niners what they were. Give us our Political
Right to share the Responsibility of Government because of our Children
and for the sake of our Constitution.

Katherine Mackay.

>25 Am.

Katherine Mackay, a suffrage leader in New York state, used her connections as
daughter-in-law of John Mackay, one of the Comstock mining kings, to promote
the cause of suffrage in Nevada. (Nevada Historical Society)

suffered from severe depression. In 1894, he shot and killed himself.

Frances Williamson had remained busy and involved in community activities in Austin after the death of her younger children. She stayed active following the death of her other son and her husband. Two months after John died, she sold the store, and dedicated herself to suffrage activities. At a meeting attended by 125 people at the Austin courthouse in late 1894, the Lucy Stone Non-Partisan Equal Suffrage League was organized. It was Nevada's first organization specifically formed to address the issue of suffrage for women. The group sponsored a letterwriting campaign and speaking tours.

There was more national encouragement in the spring of 1895 when Susan B. Anthony was once more in Nevada, accompanied by national suffrage figure, Anna Shaw. Later that year the Nevada State Equal Suffrage Association was formed in Reno, with Frances Williamson as president. Dr. J. E. Stubbs, president of the University, and an outspoken supporter of women's voting rights, presented the devotional at the meeting.

A second state suffrage convention was held in September 1896 and Frances Williamson was actively involved. She was named state organizer and lecturer. Two months later, Susan B. Anthony and Carrie Chapman Catt visited Nevada and spoke at McKissick's Opera House in Reno.

The following year, 1897, activity continued with the founding by Williamson and her daughter, Mary Laura, of *The Nevada Citizen*. The newspaper was adopted as the official voice of the Nevada State Equal Suffrage Association at the third annual convention in October 1897. The publication's stated objective, "To promote the advancement of women in the ethics of civil government, ordained in the Declaration of Independence and established by the Constitution of the United States of America." The life of the paper was brief; by 1898 Williamson had discontinued publication and moved to California with her daughter. Mary Laura Williamson died about two years after their move, and Frances Williamson, who had lost her husband and all six of her children, went on with her life. She stayed active in the suffrage movement in California.

The last effort to gain the vote in the nineteenth century was made in 1899 when a Nye County senator, George Ernst, introduced a suffrage amendment that passed in the Senate. There was no corresponding support in the Assembly. Despite some close calls, dedi-

officers elected.   At this meeting over forty seven signed the
charter list,   and we felt very much encouraged over the outlook
for a big demonstration meeting that had been discussed for the
following Saturday evening.

    From all over the State word was being received from friends
of the equal suffrage movement and the success of the meeting to be
held on Saturday at Odd Fellows hall was assured. One of the treats
of the evening was the musical program and Mrs. Elizabeth Powell-

----

1
  Officers 1911, President- Mrs. Henry Stanislawsky---- Reno.
  First Vice President----- Al G. Price-------------Rawhide.
Second   "   "   -----Mrs. O. H. Mack--------Reno.
Third   "   "   -----Miss Felice Cohn-----Carson City.
Recording Secretary------- Mrs. Frank Nicholas--Reno.
Corresponding "   ------ -Mrs. Grace Armstrong-- Reno.
Treasurer-------------Mrs. Alice Chism---------Reno.
Mrs. Chas. Bridges, J.H. Buck and Mr. Buchanan served as publicity
committee. Mrs. Mc Kinley and Judge Seeds circulated a petition.
Nevada State Journal, Jan. 24, 1911.
2
  Charter list,: J. E. Stubbs, Ella Stubbs, Alice E. Armstrong, J.
D. Layman,Jennie Blanche Taylor, Margaret Stanislawsky, C. A. Jacob-
son, Julia F. Bender, Florence H. Church, J. E. Church, Jr., Laura
de Laguna, Kate Bardenwerper, Nettie P. Hershiser, Grant Miller,
Judge Hibbard,Alice A. Chism, Mrs. Page, J. Holman Buck, C. R. Reeves,
Mrs. F. B. Patrick, Miss Mc Andrews, Mrs. A. McKinley, A. F. Price,
Mrs. O. H. Mack, Mrs. F. G. Nicholas, Miss F. Cohn, *illegible handwritten text*

*The footnote in this history of the suffrage movement provides a useful and
informative list of those involved.*
(University of Nevada, Reno, Special Collections)

cated and enthusiastic effort on the part of both women and men over three decades had failed to gain the vote. Women in other western states had been more successful. Utah Territory followed Wyoming's example and granted women the vote in 1870. Colorado granted women suffrage in 1893, Idaho in 1896. In Nevada it took a full decade more for women and men to gain sufficient momentum in the twentieth century to make a final and successful push for suffrage. Between 1899 and 1910 the suffrage movement came to a virtual standstill.

In the fall of 1910 Jeanne Weir, who was head of the department of history and political science at the University of Nevada as well as executive secretary of the Nevada Historical Society, helped launch a renewed effort to gain the vote for Nevada women when she circulated an organizational pledge among suffrage supports. Weir had received a letter the previous winter from Katherine Mackay, a New York state suffrage leader, who was the daughter-in-law of Comstock mining king John Mackay. Mrs. Mackay suggested to Weir that a branch of the Equal Franchise Society be established in Nevada. The formation of the organization was a slow process. Senator Levi Syphus, of Lincoln County, had agreed to introduce a resolution into the current legislative session, and suffrage supporters were lobbying in favor of a state constitutional amendment.

Slow though the start might have been, once the suffrage campaign was under way, it rolled forward with energy and enthusiasm. A meeting at the Odd Fellow's Hall in Reno in late January 1911 filled the assembly room there and spilled out into the lobby and stairs. Several days later Assembly Joint and Concurrent Resolution No. 6 was introduced. In February suffrage supporters took a special train, the "State House Limited," from Reno to Carson City where a number of individuals spoke before the legislature. Felice Cohn, a Carson City attorney, addressed the issue of women's legal status in Nevada.

Felice Cohn was born in Carson City in 1884. Her father was a merchant and her grandfather was Rabbi Sheyer. She was a brilliant student and she qualified for her first teaching certificate when she was eleven years old. She taught for a short period before going on to the University of Nevada, and then Stanford. She studied law, and was admitted to the bar in 1902 when she was eighteen. By 1906 she was the first woman assistant district attorney.

To the Reno Voters

I Am a Candidate for the Office of City Attorney

I regret that I cannot call upon you individually, so take this means of submitting to you my qualifications for City Attorney of Reno, Nevada.

First, I am a native of Carson City, Nevada, educated in our public schools and University of Nevada, Stanford University and George Washington Law School.

Second: Admitted to practice law in all the courts of Nevada, California and Colorado, also the United States Supreme Court.

Third: I have practiced law successfully in Carson City, Goldfield and Reno. On our entry into the War I left private practice and was appointed Special Attorney for the Government, releasing four men for service, and for five years after the war was held as Special Hearings Attorney for the General Land office, trying cases in Colorado, Oklahoma, Kansas and Nevada. Nevada cases involving title to mineral lands selected by the Railroad, and I succeeded in having more than 80,000 acres of mineral land restored to the public domain.

I returned to Nevada in 1921, and established my office in Reno, where I have remained.

Trusting this information will receive your favorable consideration on Tuesday, May 3, I am,

Yours very truly,

Felice Cohn
FOR CITY ATTORNEY
(Political Advertisement)

Political advertisement from Felice Cohn's campaign for Reno City Attorney, 1927. (Nevada State Journal, May 1, 1927)

Felice Cohn was one of the founding members of the Nevada Equal Franchise Society. She had a personal interest when she lobbied the legislature for the passage of a resolution stating: "There shall be no denial of the elective franchise at any election on account of sex." She had drafted the wording for that resolution.

Cohn continued to practice law, interested in cases involving women and children, and served three terms as U.S. Referee in Bankruptcy for the District of Nevada. She was an unsuccessful candidate for the Assembly in 1924, and also ran for Reno City Attorney in 1927, but was defeated. Her last campaign was for District Judge in 1951, and that too was a defeat. She was active in many organizations that revealed the breadth of her interests. In the final days of the suffrage struggle, however, she was a tireless and devoted worker and leader.

In 1911, opponents to the suffrage resolution hurled several procedural roadblocks into the path of the legislation that Felice Cohn had written, and managed to hold up a vote in the Assembly until March 6. More delays resulted in a week's wait for the Senate reading. The resolution was finally adopted just three days before the end of the legislative session.

Anne Martin's history of the Nevada equal suffrage campaign notes that Nevada had the smallest, most scattered population of all the states, a voting constituency that was spread out over 110,000 square miles of territory randomly speckled by cities, ranching communities, and mining towns roughly connected by ungraded dirt roads. With a transient male population, Martin calculated that there was about one voter for every five miles of Nevada's mostly desert landscape. Martin observed that suffrage supporters were aware that the success of 1911 was only a preliminary step, and that "the real battle for submission must be fought in 1913." Through the alkali dust, mud, snow, ice, heat and cold deplored by Martin, the final battle for the vote was fought across the vast expanses of Nevada.

Other western states had granted voting rights to women during the period Nevada's campaign was renewed: Washington state in 1910, California in 1911, Oregon, Arizona, and Kansas in 1912. Early in 1912 Anne Martin was elected president of the Nevada Equal Franchise Society, and throughout the year county societies were organized. By early 1913, eleven county societies listed a total of 500 paid members.

HOW SUFFRAGE SPEECHMAKERS KNOCK NEVADA

State Is Given Reputation of Being Vicious and Wild In the East

EFFECT OF SUCH TALK EXPOSED BY BOSTONIAN

Mrs. Leatherbee Tells Why She Is Opopsed to Votes For Women

Mrs. Jewett W. Adams of Carson City, president of the Nevada Association of Women Opposed to Equal Suffrage, arrived in town this afternoon direct from Virginia City where she was campaigning in the cause of Anti-Suffrage.

Mrs. Adams is accompanied by Mrs. Albert T. Leatherbee, of Boston, who spoke at the opera house at Virginia last night to a large and enthusiastic audience.

Mrs. Leatherbee was introduced by Hon. William Ryan, county clerk of Story county, as one of the "Boston Braves," and opened her remarks by saying that Boston people considered her brave to come to Nevada and advised her to pack a gun; because they had constantly heard the suffrage speakers declaiming on the vicious condition of Nevada, which they claimed was the center of all the vice that had been driven from the purified woman-suffrage states around them into man-suffrage Nevada.

Mrs. Leatherbee did not consider this very good advertising for the state and thought Nevada might get along very nicely without any such suffrage boosting. Mrs. Adams appears very much pleased with the outlook in Storey and Ormsby counties and says that after all the years she has lived in this state and the knowledge she has of Nevada men, she cannot believe they will be so lacking in chivalry and justice as to force the ballot upon 97 per cent of the adult women to please the passing whim of 3 per cent.

Nevada's anti-suffrage leaders launched a vigorous campaign against votes for women (Nevada Historical Society)

THE NEVADA ASSOCIATION OF WOMEN
OPPOSED TO EQUAL SUFFRAGE

RENO, NEVADA, July 3, 1914.

Hon. Woodrow Wilson,

The White House,

Washington, D. C.

Sir:—

At a meeting of the Nevada Association of Women Opposed to Equal Suffrage, the State Chairman was directed to communicate to the President, the Governor, the Senators and Representative from Nevada their protest against the proposed extension of the franchise to women by amendment to the Federal Constitution. The reasons prompting this protest are:

We believe the strength of the Nation lies in the home and the family. We find the leaders in every element of society opposed to the institutions urging women into politics. We find these leaders in recognized positions of conspicuous leadership in the movement for Equal Suffrage. If their reasoning be sound, their success means to us the weakening, if not the downfall of the home, the family and the Nation, regardless of the views of many good women supporting the movement.

In Colorado, the only state where time, population and general conditions have afforded a test, we find, after twenty years a disappointment for every promise. In lieu of government we find anarchy; in lieu of order chaos; in lieu of home rule, Federal control; in lieu of economy in government the highest per capita tax rate of any State; we find, with but two exceptions, its capital and principal city with the highest per capita expense of those in its class; in lieu of improved domestic conditions we find but two states in 48 with a higher divorce rate; we find the social evil aggravated, not abated.

Few women pay taxes. The proposed amendment would multiply the proportion of non tax-paying voters and practically double the number of those who could vote away the income and further tax the women already taxed, without themselves sharing the burden.

In nine states women now have the full franchise. If the experience of Colorado is to be the experience of the other eight states, it will be and should be rejected by those states which examine first and approve afterward, and no state or group of states should force this experiment upon another. If the claims in its behalf be confirmed by experience its adoption by general consent will follow, welcomed by the women of Nevada as of other states.

The only preferential or test vote in any state by which the women could express their own wish was in Massachusetts in 1895, where 22,204 out of an estimated total of 850,000, or 1 in 38, expressed a desire for the franchise. Two other states already had equal suffrage by the votes of men.

We are informed that Congress has been petitioned "in the name of the women of Nevada" and that the President has been urged, to advocate an extension of the franchise by amendment of the Federal constitution, notwith-

Anti-suffrage groups pursued their own campaign. (Nevada Historical Society)

MRS. OLIPHANT'S ADDRESS

Mrs. O. D. Oliphant of New Jersey will speak at the Majestic Theater Saturday evening at 8 o'clock under the auspices of the Nevada Association of Women Opposed to Equal Suffrage. Admission free, everybody invited. 3t

Like suffrage supporters, the anti-suffrage campaign looked for support outside the state. (Nevada Historical Society)

WOMEN UNDER NEVADA LAWS

By B. M. Wilson

The inequalities of men and women under the law in Nevada are apparent by a reading of the statutes. And although Nevada is more liberal in its treatment of women than many States, there is still unjust discrimination between the rights of women and the rights of men, and this will never be remedied until the women themselves have power to make laws. They will then be in a position to reform, not only such laws as are unjust to women, but those that affect the welfare of the entire community.

Is It Right?

Women are tax-payers. Women are citizens, according to the courts. Women are half the people.

Is it right that half the people, only, should do all the voting? The United States is not a Democracy, and government by "the people" has never been tried in Nevada. Taxation without representation is tyranny, now as it was in 1776.

Nevada Has No Votes for Women.

Not even school suffrage is granted to the women of Nevada. Thirty States give some form of votes to women. Three of these are tax-paying suffrage; three are school and tax-paying suffrage; eighteen have some form of school suffrage; one has municipal suffrage; SIX have votes for men and women on equal terms. Why not Nevada?

What Offices Can Women Hold?

By election, only those of Superintendent of Public Schools and School Trustee (Art. XV., Sec. 3, Constitution). But women rarely get these positions, in Nevada. The politicians need them for stepping-stones, so the man with a vote secures the place, while the woman without a vote does not.

Premium on Remaining Single.

The laws at present tend to turn thinking women away from marriage.

The unmarried woman suffers no injustice as to property rights. She may hold property, engage in business, and will property as freely as a man. She may also relinquish her citizenship (gained by birth or inherited from her one legal parent), and enroll as a citizen in the country of her choice.

Marriage gives to a woman the citizenship of her husband; if he is a foreigner, she also becomes one.

Marriage destroys woman's legal individuality. It even takes away her name, and effaces her identity.

Marriage takes away the control of her earnings, and

Motherhood does not give her the control of her children.

Separate Property.

A wife may hold separate property, if she had it before marriage, and that which she may afterwards receive by gift or inheritance. This may be kept in her name alone, and wholly under her control, by filing an inventory of the same in the county where she resides, and where the property is situated. (Secs. 2155 and 2159, Revised laws.) To neglect this matter of recording is to subject the property to the debts of her husband.

Community Property.

All earnings of husband and wife are called "community property." This sounds well, but is a complete misnomer. The property so earned is absolutely controlled by the husband, as long as he lives. He may sell it without the consent of the wife, and may will away half of it, thus controlling it even after death. (Secs. 2156 and 2160, Rev. Laws.)

Bird Wilson compiled and wrote this tract on women and the law. (Nevada Historical Society)

VOTES FOR WOMEN

Legislative Candidates from whom written replies have been received, pledging themselves to vote to pass the woman suffrage amendment on to the electorate for adoption or rejection at the next General Election.

FOR THE SENATE

W. H. Cordill	James Gault	W. D. Jones
Socialist	Independent	Democrat

FOR THE ASSEMBLY

DEMOCRATS	REPUBLICANS

DEMOCRATS

Geo. N. BACHENBERG A. J. MELVILLE
W. M. GARDINER   J. P. MORRILL
J. W. GEROW   R. M. PRESTON
WM. L. HACKER

REPUBLICANS

F. R. BYRAN   A. W. HOLMES
R. A. GOTT   J. LOZANO
FRED B. HART   GEO. F. TRANTER
J. L. HASH   JOHN W. WRIGHT
        G. E. HOLESWORTH

PROGRESSIVES

BENJAMIN CURLER C. A. RICHARDSON
C. M. NEASHAM   FRANK SAVAGE
GEO. PECKHAM   ISIDORE WOOD

SOCIALISTS

C. J. BECHER   C. W. GALLOWAY
J. T. BRENNAN   A. GRANT MILLER
C. W. FARRINGTON ANDREW SOLARI
        JUD HARRIS

Vote For These Men who have given their pledge to help free the women of Nevada, that NEVADA may rank with the six other States where women have this human right: CALIFORNIA, COLORADO, IDAHO, UTAH, WASHINGTON AND WYOMING.

Votes For Women in Nevada in 1914

Published by the **NEVADA EQUAL FRANCHISE SOCIETY**

NOVEMBER 2, 1912   139 North Virginia Street, Reno

A blitz of information attempted to persuade voters. (Nevada Historical Society)

NEVADA NEXT!

☐ Equal Suffrage for Women.
▨ Partial Suffrage for Women.
■ No Suffrage for Women.

WOMEN HAVE FULL SUFFRAGE IN ALL WHITE STATES

Wyoming Granted Suffrage to Women in 1869; Colorado in 1893; Utah in 1896; Idaho in 1896; Washington in 1910; California in 1911; Oregon, Arizona and Kansas in 1912.

Illinois Gave Presidential, Partial County, State and Full Municipal Suffrage to Women in 1913.
Alaska Women Were Enfranchised in 1913.

The States Where the Woman Suffrage Amendment Will Be Voted On November, 1914, Are Ohio, Montana, Nebraska, Missouri, North and South Dakota and NEVADA.

WHY NOT MAKE NEVADA A WHITE STATE, TOO?

CONSIDER THESE FACTS

THE POPULATION OF NEVADA IS OVER 80,000, of which 40,000 are men over 21 years of age and 18,000 are women. (Census of 1910.)

OF THESE 40,000 MEN, owing to transitory occupations in Nevada, on an average only 20,000 remain in the state long enough to vote, and of these 20,000 voters fully 50 per cent is estimated to be transient or "floating."

OF NEVADA'S 18,000 WOMEN ONLY 20 PER CENT IS ESTIMATED TO BE TRANSIENT, as our women have permanent occupations as mothers and housewives on the farms and in the homes of the state. When the women of Nevada have the vote, that part of the population that has the permanent interests of the state at heart, the "home builders" among men and women, will be increased by many thousands of votes, and the influence of the stable population in lawmaking will inevitably promote the interests of industry and agriculture, of our schools and our children.

NEVADA HAS THE HIGHEST PERCENTAGE OF MALE POPULATION and the largest proportionate transient vote in the United States. NEVADA HAS THE LOWEST PERCENTAGE OF WOMEN IN POPULATION IN THE UNITED STATES. The history of the world shows that no state can build up permanent homes and develop farming and agriculture without the help of women. Therefore, progress and self interest demand that we make Nevada an inviting state for women to come to, a state which gives women equal citizenship with men, instead of one which, as now, deprives women of political liberty the instant they cross our borders from any of the free states by which we are entirely surrounded.

MEN OF NEVADA, if you are working for the advancement of the true interests of the state,

GIVE VOTES TO NEVADA WOMEN!

NEVADA WOMEN SHOULD VOTE BECAUSE

...ince this is a government of the People, by the People and for the
        VOTES FOR WOMEN
...ince they are concerned equally with the men in good or bad govern-
...or civic righteousness. Justice demands   VOTES FOR WOMEN
...nd by payment of direct tax on property and indirect taxes on food
...mes of the government. Since taxation without representation is
        VOTES FOR WOMEN
...RE (more than 8,000,000 women in the United States are working
... hours of labor and their conditions of work depend upon the laws,
        VOTES FOR WOMEN
...since the ballot helps to control sanitary and moral conditions that sur-

...mands Votes For Women

... idiots, Indians and Chinamen (except as enfranchised by federal reg-
...WOMEN are not allowed to vote?
...ne form of suffrage to women, but that not even school suffrage is

... "community property" earned by the combined efforts of husband
... by the husband as long as he lives, that he may sell it without the
... of it, thus controlling it even after death, but if the wife dies first,
... of it by will? (Secs. 2156 and 2160 Revised Laws.)

...ife possessed before marriage or which she receives afterwards by gift
... of her husband, UNLESS she keeps it in her own name and under
...ntory of the property in the county where she resides and ....ere the
... and 2156 Revised Laws.)

...w the wife's signature to deeds of property is not ......ary except
...eclared?
... husband absolutely controls his 'wife's earnings, and can take them
...em in penury?
... of her husband when he cannot support himself, and that her separate
...red in this support? (Sec. 2178 Rev. Laws.)
... with the father the estate of a child where no will is made? (Laws

... has been passed for men working underground, in mills, plaster works,
...in dispatchers, there is no law applying to the labor of woman and she
...any hours as her employer decides?

... Nevada is sixteen years? A girl cannot legally sell her property at
...er virtue. (Sec. 2339 Revised Laws.)

... the penalty for stealing a girl for immoral purposes is imprison-
...,000, while for stealing a horse or a mule the thief may be imprisoned
...ev. Laws.)

...ment of the constitution amendment permitting women to vote has
... in 1911, and again in 1913 with only three dissenting votes in each

...ENT WILL BE SUBMITTED TO THE MALE ELECTORATE FOR
...XT ELECTION ON NOVEMBER 3 OF THIS YEAR.

...'T KEEP YOUR WOMEN OUT!

...men Ought To Give Their Help
... Ought To Have Their Help
... State Ought to Use Their Help

...nfranchisement of Nevada women is asked to write for suffrage lit-
...nt cards and to send a campaign contribution to

STATE HEADQUARTERS

EQUAL FRANCHISE SOCIETY

...g   153 NORTH VIRGINIA STREET, RENO, NEVADA

First Ed

OUT WEST

AUGUST   1914

The Clash in Nevada

A History of
Woman's Fight
For Enfranchisement

THE NEVADA ſUFFRAGE FIGHT

Articles by

Jane Addams
Mrs. Charlotte Perkins Gilman   Sara Bard Field
Mrs Carrie Chapman Catt   Inez Haynes Gillmore
Mrs. Mary Roberts Coolidge   Gail Laughlin
Mary Austin and Anne Martin   Dr. Anna Howard Shaw

Out West, *August 1914. Prominent national leaders for suffrage were involved in the Nevada campaign. (Ormsby Public Library)*

No Picketing

…VADA EQUAL FRANCHISE SOCIETY HAS
… THE MEMBERS OF THE ORGANIZATION
…OUT THE STATE TO "PICKET THE POLLS"
…TION DAY.

…MONY WITH THE POLICY OF THE NEVADA
…TION OF WOMEN OPPOSED TO EQUAL SUF-
…RESPECTFULLY ASK THAT NO WOMEN IN
…Y WITH ITS OBJECTS APPEAR AT OR NEAR
…S ON ELECTION DAY, TRUSTING TO THE
…NEVADA TO PROTECT THE WOMEN OF THE
…OM THE NECESSITY OF ACTIVE PARTICI-
…N POLITICS OR POLITICAL CAMPAIGNS.

    MRS. J. W. ADAMS, State Chairman ——

…NEVADA ASSOCIATION OF WOMEN
——OPPOSED TO EQUAL SUFFRAGE—
…E STREET   RENO, NEVADA

The women of the anti-suffrage association asked the women of Nevada to trust the "men of Nevada to protect the women of the home from the necessity of active participation in politics." Emma Lee Adams, wife of a former governor, was strongly opposed to women voting. (Nevada Historical Society)

The Last Word
AGAINST
WOMAN SUFFRAGE

BY
Miss Minnie Bronson
—OF NEW YORK——
General Secretary of National
Asso. opposed to woman suffrage

TONIGHT

Free Picture Show - Speaking
at eight o'clock - Everybody
Welcome - Admission FREE
and NO Collection

—— UNDER AUSPICES ——
Nevada Association of Women
Opposed to Equal Suffrage

UNIVERSITY OF NEVADA BULLETIN

| Vol. XLII | AUGUST 1948 | No. 7 |

The Story of the Nevada Equal Suffrage Campaign

Memoirs of Anne Martin

❧

Edited with introduction and notes by Austin E. Hutcheson, History
Department, University of Nevada

❧

PUBLISHED QUARTERLY BY THE UNIVERSITY OF NEVADA
RENO, NEVADA

Entered in the Post Office at Reno, Nevada, as second-class matter under Act
of Congress, July 16, 1894. Acceptance for mailing at special rate of
postage provided for in section 1103, Act of October 3, 1917, authorized
April 21, 1919.
1⁷⁹

*This suffrage newspaper consolidated much of the information about suffrage
issues. (Nevada Historical Society)*

National women's leaders continued to tour in support of state efforts. Activist Charlotte Perkins Gilman spoke in southern Nevada, where she was booed when she refused to share a stage with Senator Francis Newlands. She received an enthusiastic welcome, however, from a Reno audience at the Majestic Theater.

The suffrage amendment was introduced again to the legislature and Governor Tasker Oddie urged passage. Both the Senate and Assembly overwhelmingly passed the measure. The suffrage amendment was scheduled for the ballot in November, 1914. Nevada had 23,000 voters, with more than half those in the rural counties. Campaign workers used voter registration lists obtained from county clerks, believing that it was necessary to get suffrage literature to every voter in the state, but particularly important in the rural areas. Anne Martin anticipated resistance to suffrage from the cities. There, she believed, "big business," the gambling and saloon interests held sway.

Resistance came from more than the saloon interests in Nevada. In 1913 an anti-suffrage league was formed, led by Mrs. Emma Lee Adams, wife of former governor Jewett Adams. This group, too, imported national leaders to support their position. Miss Minnie Bronson of New York and Mrs. J. D. Oliphant of New Jersey toured the state. George Wingfield, an important financial and political figure in Nevada, had come out against suffrage, and contributed to the outside campaigners. Anne Martin noted that, in contrast to the hardships encountered by the pro-suffrage campaigners, the antis "were provided with every obtainable luxury and the meetings were remarkably well advertised and arranged. They undoubtedly were supported by the liquor and other vested interests." Martin and her supporters campaigned throughout the state in rented Model Ts, making only fifteen miles a day on some of the rough and rutted roads; traveling to a settlement or ranchhouse by evening if possible, but sleeping out in the desert when it was not.

1914 was a busy campaign year for Martin and many others who worked to canvass the state town-by-town and neighborhood-by-neighborhood. May 2 was declared Women's Independence Day and women's groups sponsored pageants, processions, and speakers. Also in May, suffrage supporters declared "self-denial week" when women denied themselves small luxuries—visits to the theater, new gloves and hats, ice cream and candy, and dress ornaments—then gave the money they saved to county suffrage societies.

Taking to the streets in gaily decorated floats, suffrage supporters advised citizens, "Don't Keep Your Women Out." (University of Nevada, Reno, Special Collections)

Record Courier, *October 16, 1914, Jane Addams, well known for her social work at Hull House in Chicago, supported women's suffrage and came to Nevada to publicly speak in support of the vote.*

MISS JANE ADDAMS

Jane Addams To Speak at Reno

Miss Jane Addams will speak on suffrage at the Majestic Theatre, in Reno on Sunday afternoon, October 18th at 3 o'clock.

Miss Jane Addams, generally known as "Jane Addams of Hull House" was born at Cedarville, Illinois, September 8, 1860. She was a delicate child, and and this delicacy made her thoughtful beyond her years, and did much to determine the trend of her later life. She was graduated from Rockford College, Illinois and has taken post graduate courses in this country and in Europe, receiving he degree of Doctor of Laws from the University of Wisconsin, and the degree of Master of Arts from Smith College in 1910. Since leaving college Miss Addams has given her life to social reforms, and has brought to this work a singleness of purpose and a sympathy that have earned her the love and respect of every civilized nation. In 1889 with Miss Ellen Gates Starr, she founded Hull House in Chicago, of which for the first she has been head resident. Hull House has long been recognized as the most successful exponent of the social settlement idea, and has given a better idea of life to the people of Chicago's most crowded slums. Miss Addams is an extremely busy woman, for, besides personally supervising the complex life that centers in Hull House, she is a constant worker for municipal reform and social betterment in Chicago, has been active in securing laws for the benefit of factory employees, and for the suppression of the white slave traffic. Her interest in the welfare of humanity extends also to woman suffrage, and she has become one of the greatest and most efficient leaders in the movement. She is also the author of several books, of which the best known is "Twenty Years at Hull House."

Jane Addams has a sweet and most winning personality. She has the heart of a mother, and is in fact a mother whose children are the weak and the unfortunate, and whose home for all who are in need. Miss Addams' face is marked with the sadness that comes to those who have seen much suffering, but her eyes look hopefully upon the world that she is always trying to help.

WESTERN UNION TELEGRAM

NEWCOMB CARLTON, PRESIDENT
GEORGE W. E. ATKINS, VICE-PRESIDENT   BELVIDERE BROOKS, VICE-PRESIDENT

RECEIVED AT
A57 SF TA 69 COLLECT NL

RENO NEV MAY 12 15

PRESS BUREAU EMPIRE STATE CAMPAIGN COMMITTEE
CR MRS CARRIE CHAPMAN CATT 303 5 AVE NY CITY
REPLYING REQUEST INFORMATION WOMANS VOTE   RENO ELECTION SALOONS AND
ANTIS DEFEATED SUFFRAGE IN RENO   BY SIX HUNDRED VOTES SALOONS ANTIS-
UFFRAGISTS AND SOME GOOD MEN AND WOMEN DEFEATED PROPOSED DRASTIC
SALOON ORDINANCE MAY FOURTH REDUCING   NUMBER LIQUOR LICENSES FROM
EIGHTY TO FORTY SOME VOTERS   FAVORING PROHIBITION VOTED AGAINST
ORDINANCE NINETY PERCENT REGISTERED WOMEN VOTED EIGHTY PERCENT
REGISTERED MEN ,MEN NEARLY TWO TO ONE WOMEN VOTED RAPIDLY INTELLI-
GENTLY WITHOUT MISTAKES
                ANNE H MARTIN   543AM

Anne Martin stayed in touch with national supporters. (Nevada Historical Society)

WOMEN OF RENO
You Are Now Citizens
Entitled To Vote
in the
CITY ELECTION, MAY 4
The registration office is at the City
Hall and is open daily from 10 A.M.
to 6 P.M. and from 7 P.M. to 9 P.M.

Registration Closes April 23rd at 6 P.M.
REGISTER NOW
and help elect the Clean Government Ticket

With success, former suffrage activists had a further goal: to educate the new voters. (Nevada Historical Society)

I BELIEVE in Woman's Suffrage.

I ALSO believe that cleanliness is next to godliness; therefore I am in the laundry business.

Our Work Is Always Satisfactory

E. J. STEVENS

Proprietor Troy Power Laundry

Some business people weren't above using suffrage to sell laundry services. (Nevada Historical Society)

WOMEN SHOULD POSSESS THE BALLOT, AS MEN DO, BECAUSE, HAVING EQUAL RESPONSIBILITY FOR THE PUBLIC WELFARE, THEY SHOULD HAVE EQUAL OPPORTUNITY AND POWER FOR PUBLIC SERVICE.

Pennsylvania Men's League for Woman Suffrage

HONORARY PRESIDENT	Office, Farm Journal Building, Washington Square	HON. VICE-PRESIDENTS
DIMNER BEEBER	(First floor, left corridor, 2d door to right)	RABBI JOS. KRAUSKOPF, PHILA.
		WILLIAM DRAPER LEWIS, PHILA.
HON. VICE-PRESIDENTS	MOVE ON, MEN; MOVE ON!	FRANK E. MORGAN, PHILA.
DR. LEO S. ROWE, PHILA.		VANCE C. McCORMICK
JULIAN KENNEDY, ESQ., PITTSBURGH		JEREMIAH J. SULLIVAN, JR., PHILA.
RT. REV. JAMES H. DARLINGTON,	PRESIDENT SECRETARY TREASURER	ARTHUR E. HUTCHINSON, PHILA.
HARRISBURG	WILMER ATKINSON MRS. FRED'K E. DRINKER HENRY JUSTICE	DR. GEO. WOODWARD, PHILA.
HON. GIFFORD PINCHOT, PHILA.		MORRIS L. COOKE, PHILA.
GEO. BURNHAM, JR., PHILA.	CAMPAIGN COMMITTEE	ROY SMITH WALLACE, PHILA.
REV. CARL E. GRAMMER, PHILA.	JOHN M. SHRIGLEY, RYERSON W. JENNINGS	SHIPPEN LEWIS, PHILA.
J. LEVERING JONES, PHILA.	FERDINAND H. GRASER, GEO. C. SMALL	ALFRED H. GRANGER, PHILA.
DR. JOHN G. CLARK, PHILA.	HENRY J. GIBBONS AND JOHN JAY RIDGWAY	

EXECUTIVE SECRETARY
ARTHUR M. DEWEES

9

PHILADELPHIA, SEPTEMBER, 1915.

Dear Sir:-

There is a wide spread desire in states where woman suffrage is to be voted on this fall to know how it works in your state, and I address you in hopes of obtaining from you a brief statement in regard to the matter. Those opposed to women voting persist in declaring:

That it will make men less chivalrous, less respectful to women;
That it will unsex women and detract from their charm;
That all bad women will vote and many good women will not;
That woman's place is in the home--the inference being that the home will be broken up. This is the major objection and is supposed to settle the matter.
That the indirect influence they exert over their husbands, and upon such public affairs as interest them, is all sufficient without the ballot, in fact
That Equal Suffrage is a failure in your state, as in other states where it has had trial.

What is your answer to these allegations. May I have it briefly with your photograph? A symposium from Governors, covering the ground as indicated, will be of great interest to many here who are seeking light.

Very respectfully,

Wilmer Atkinson President.
Pennsylvania Men's League for Woman Suffrage.

To Governor Emmet D. Boyle,

Nevada.

WA/E

LOOK AT THE MAP.—No better proof that Woman Suffrage is successful is needed than that it has been marching eastward in solid phalanx, one State after another adopting it. A State tries the just experiment, and adjoining States, seeing its benefits, do the same. Were "Votes for Women" a failure, it would present an example for contiguous States to leave it alone. Nowhere has it failed. The Keystone State should take the hint and give fair play to women on November Second, 1915. Register September 2nd, 7th, or 11th.

Suffrage supporters in states that did not yet have women voting, turned to states that had granted women the franchise for information and advice.

Women participated in the Reno Fourth of July parade with a float decorated in white and yellow flowers. Winnemucca had a suffrage tea where everyone learned the tango, and Lovelock sponsored a suffrage dance where they handed out "Votes for Women" buttons.

Letter writing campaigns sent personal letters to every state candidate, and suffrage supporters from other states visited and spoke for the Nevada cause. In September and October, Antoinette Funk from Chicago, and Margaret Foley from Boston came to help. Dr. Anna Howard Shaw addressed an audience of 1200 at the Majestic Theater in Reno, and also toured to Carson City, Virginia City, Tonopah, Goldfield, Las Vegas, and Caliente. Jane Addams of Chicago's Hull House fame, traveled to speak in Elko, Winnemucca, and Reno.

In November the massive effort came to a successful completion when women gained the vote. The statewide tally was 10,936 for and 7,258 opposed. As Anne Martin had predicted, the urban areas, Washoe, Ormsby, Storey, and Eureka counties, voted against women's suffrage. The vote was won in the dusty, isolated mining camps, and small towns scattered across sparsely settled Nevada.

After passage of the suffrage amendment in Nevada a number of individuals and political figures in other states wrote to Governor Emmet Boyle requesting information about the impact of voting women on Nevada society. One memorable letter from the president of the Pennsylvania Men's League for Woman Suffrage presented a list of arguments made by anti-suffrage groups—one being that "all bad women will vote and many good women will not"—and asked the governor to comment on the allegations. In a letter dated September 22, 1915, Boyle replied that woman suffrage in Nevada was too recent to have been given a real trial. He had, however, observed the situation in neighboring states and concluded, "Women appear to exercise their voice in public affairs with benefit to those communities in which the system is in force and with no sacrifice of their domestic qualities."

With achievement of the long sought goal—the vote—women shifted focus and worked to educate voters. There was significant interconnection for women among specific issues. The success with the suffrage effort provided a springboard for electing women to political office. It would take decades for women to attain power and influence as elected political figures, but they swiftly pursued those goals once they gained the vote and a legally efficacious political voice.

Hannah Clapp, photograph by J.H. Wykoff.
In the nineteenth century, before women gained the vote and a
number of political rights, Hanna Clapp lobbied male politicians
to gain political power. (Nevada Historical Society)

WOMEN AND POLITICS IN NEVADA

When state and federal constitutions were amended to grant women the vote in Nevada in 1914 and nationally in 1919, women entered a new age. Entitled now to vote, to hold elected office, and to serve on juries, the prospects for enacting social change seemed endless and exciting, and women pursued their new opportunities enthusiastically. The right to assert themselves through the ballot box was the culmination of a century of effort, but political activism was not a new concept for American women. Women in Nevada and across the nation had been politically active long before they acquired the right to vote.

Initial political activity came from within the family. As mothers of sons who were future participants in the democratic process, political activity was indirect but socially significant. Women continued indirect public participation in the political process throughout the nineteenth century by joining in demonstrations, sponsoring rallies, circulating petitions, marching in parades, and lobbying for various causes. The influence of women in major political causes—abolition, temperance, and suffrage—before they received the vote was profound.

Hannah Keziah Clapp was a politically active woman in nineteenth-century Nevada. Born in upstate New York, Clapp came overland with her family to California, then moved to Carson City in 1860. Her political skills were evident early on. She used her friendship with Senator William Stewart to lobby for a bill in the 1861 Territorial Legislature to create a school in Carson City, which later became her Sierra Seminary. Two years later she wrote to Governor Nye requesting an appropriation for her school. Her political contacts gained her appointments in 1883 as Assembly Committee Clerk and Senate Copy Clerk in 1885. When the Comstock slumped and she lost money on mining investments, Hannah Clapp prevailed upon

Sarah Winnemucca, ca. 1880, was a well-known and controversial figure. Her celebrity and public status was remarkable for a woman of her time, particularly so for a Native American woman. (Nevada Historical Society)

political friendships to obtain a position with the University when it moved to Reno from Elko in 1886. She stayed at the University until her retirement in 1901. Hannah Clapp continued her friendship with Stewart, and was perceived as an important conduit for political patronage. Her correspondence with him indicates that she kept him informed about political developments in Nevada, and he passed along information for her to disseminate. Denied the right to be an active part of the political process as a voter or legislator, Hannah Clapp used the system to her advantage by cultivating powerful political connections with men who could use their influence on her behalf.

Sarah Winnemucca was another politically active women in early Nevada. She was a Northern Paiute who was born around 1844, about the time that large numbers of Euro-American emigrants began to travel through the territory that would become Nevada. It was a sparse landscape where bands of native people survived in a fragile balance with nature. That balance, where small families or bands hunted and gathered over large areas, was upset by the incursion of the miners, soldiers, ranchers, merchants, and various sojourners who invaded the Native American homelands. Sarah, who was self-educated, acted as a mediator between her people and the Anglo newcomers to the Great Basin. In dramatic lectures around the country, she spoke out against the injustices endured by the natives at the hands of dishonest reservation agents. During her first visit to Washington she met with President Hayes, and petitioned the Interior Department to relieve the suffering of her people.

In 1880, Sarah Winnemucca again traveled to Washington, D.C. with her brother and father to meet with the Secretary of the Interior on behalf of the Paiutes and other native bands. Promises made to her and her people in meetings with Washington officials were not fulfilled. Three years later she presented the injustices suffered by her people to a wider audience when she published *Life Among the Piutes, Their Wrongs and Claims*, which was edited by Mrs. Horace Mann. During another trip to Washington in 1884, she spoke before a congressional subcommittee on Indian affairs to plead for federal lands for a tribal reservation.

Sarah Winnemucca has been a controversial figure, reviled by some, praised by others. Gae Whitney Canfield's *Sarah Winnemucca of the Northern Paiutes* provides accounts of Winnemucca's conflict with one Indian agent who publicly questioned her virtue and truth-

Preamble and Resolutions

OF THE

Woman's * Silver * League,

TO F

Austin, Lander County, Nevada.

Adopted August 11th, 1893.

Woman's Silver League, Preamble and Resolutions
Even without the vote, women managed to assert their political views.
(University of Nevada, Reno, Special Collections)

fulness. Newspapers speculated on the number of husbands she had married. She sometimes drank to excess, and she physically attacked a man she believed had stolen money from her. Some Native Americans accused her of selling out; others viewed her as a "princess," and tribal savior. Euro-Americans had similar mixed impressions.

As a woman living in two worlds, however, both of which were changing rapidly, her advocacy was a remarkable achievement. As a Native American woman, she faced a double challenge to her political effectiveness. Discrimination based on race was as prevalent in the political sphere as it was in the private sector.

Women had begun to overcome gender bias by 1918 when Sadie Hurst, discussed below, was elected to the legislature. Political recognition of women of color was much slower, however; it was not until 1994 that Bernice Mathews, an African-American woman from Washoe County, breached that particular barrier when she was elected state senator.

Motivated to action by issues that troubled them, women were politically active and effective in the decades before they achieved the vote. The clubs and various organized groups, discussed in earlier chapters, amplified the power of a single woman's voice. In 1889, for example, Mrs. Lucy Van Deventer, president of the Nevada WCTU, wrote letters to newspapers to protest the legalization of lotteries. She also organized the members of the WCTU in the protest. The women's political activism helped to defeat the lottery bill.

A constitutional amendment in 1889 authorized women to hold the elected offices of school superintendent and school trustee. The following year women were elected to a number of those positions in Nevada school districts. Elko County elected Mrs. Josephine Taylor as school superintendent, and Mrs. Susan Miller won the post in Humboldt County. All of the trustees elected to the Galena and Lewis districts in Lander County were women, and the Hamilton district, in White Pine County also elected a woman to a trustee position. In a culture that understood women as nurturers and as morally superior to men, responsibilities for education were often thought of as an extension of women's natural talents, the role of mother expanded into the public sphere. Granting women the right to be elected to an educational office, then, was not a radical move, more like a political baby step for women. The giant step was two decades in the future.

PREAMBLE AND RESOLUTIONS.

To the Honorable Senators and Members of the House of Representatives.

WHEREAS, we the members of the Woman's Silver League of Austin, Lander County, Nevada, fully realizing that the signs of the times demand our ablest thoughts and efforts, not alone in the industrial and educational, but also in the financial world of to-day; consequently, we emphatically declare ourselves in favor of the restoration of silver to that standard which was for so many years accepted as the settled policy of the world. We firmly believe that the present depression in business, and in all industries is due to the demonetization of silver in 1873. By that covert act, the miner is deprived of the just reward for his labor; his inability to purchase the products of the farmer and manufacturer, has caused a depression in trade, which largely effects the self-supporting women in the silver producing States; hence we deem it the duty of the women of these states, to co-operate with all other Woman's Leagues who are seeking to wrest themselves and future generations from the remorseless grasp of the political, and the monied manipulators, who continually and persistently violate those constitutional principles —freedom and equality— which have made us the most practical, and the most progressive people in the world's history; therefore, be it

Resolved, that this League unanimously declare themselves in favor of the free coinage of silver at the ratio of 16, to 1 and that we con-

demn the action of our government in adopting and following the financial policy of England—a government run in the interest of nobles, landlords, bankers and capitalists for their own class exclusively, while ours is a government, "of the people, by the people, and for the people."

Resolved, that this League favor the use of silver, and that we insist on its being paid to us in all business transactions, thus giving practical evidence, that as Americans we have confidence in the products of our mines, thereby throwing the *lie* in the face of the foreign financiers, who claim that, while we *howl* silver we will not use it.

Resolved, that this League considers the action of President Cleveland on the silver question, to be in direct contradiction of those sacred principles, which has placed him in the highest office in the gift of the people of these United States.

Resolved, that copies of the preamble and resolutions, now adopted, with a letter calling attention to the same, be sent to our Representatives in Congress, also to Mrs. Cleveland, Mrs. Potter Palmer, the Woman's Industrial League of America, and to the leading papers on the Pacific coast.

All of which is respectfully submitted.

MRS. J. A. MILLER, President.

Attest: MISS MARY EGAN, Secretary.

Committee {
Mrs. J. R. Williamson,
Mrs. O. J. Clifford,
Mrs. Wm. Foster,
Mrs. W. J. McGlew,
Mrs. Thos. H. Dalton,
Miss Katie Laughlin,
Mrs. Wm. Easton.

Woman's Silver League, (University of Nevada, Reno, Special Collections)

In 1893 the Women's Silver League was organized in Austin, Nevada. The demonetization of silver, ordered by the federal government in 1873, was part of a bitterly contested program to resolve American money issues. In the wake of the Civil War, establishing a stable and uniform currency was an important goal of the national political agenda. Business interests, bankers and other creditors among them, tended to support a restricted currency based on the gold standard. Agricultural, labor, and manufacturing interests, who tended to be the debtor segment of society, supported an expanded currency. More money in circulation would tend to keep interest rates low and prices higher, the opposite of a tight money situation. Silver miners in Nevada and other western states opposed the gold standard, and supported the coinage of silver as a way to keep silver prices high and stable. In their resolution, addressed to members of Congress, the Women's Silver League decried the demonetization of silver. The 1873 Coinage Act, commonly known as "the Crime of '73," decreed that the U. S. Mint would suspend the minting of silver coins. Many mining and agricultural interests, and the women's Silver League, blamed economic hard times in the mid-1890s on the gold standard. They maintained that the depression affected

> . . . the self-supporting women in the silver producing States; hence we deem it the duty of the women of these states, to co-operate with all other Woman's Leagues who are seeking to wrest themselves and future generations from the remorseless grasp of the political, and the monied manipulators . . .

The women were expressing a commonly held political belief of the period, and participating in a significant political issue of the 1890s.

Political appointments were another source of power for women without the vote. In 1899 the legislature created a Board of Medical Examiners, a group of physicians with the power to assess the competency and to license physicians practicing medicine in Nevada. Dr. Philopena Wagner, a female physician, was among the first five physicians appointed to the Board by Governor Reinhold Sadler. Dr. Wagner was given the short-term appointment and it was years before another female physician was appointed. This reflected the step back that women in medicine were forced to take by the second decade of the twentieth century. Female physicians had been making forward progress in the nineteenth century, but better organization of the medical field resulted in barriers for women. The percentage of women physicians peaked in 1910 and then declined again until

BOMBARDING SOLONS FOR DIVORCE CHANGE

Women of City Take Initiative and Are Circulating Petitions and Swamping the Legislators With Letters

URGE CHANGE TO YEAR'S RESIDENCE

Clergymen Take up Campaign and Will Speak From Pulpits on Subject—Delegation to Go to Carson City

Many women of Reno, aided by the clergy and prominent business men, have entered upon a whirlwind campaign to force an amendment to the present divorce law of Nevada which will make the term of residence of those seeking divorce one year instead of six months.

The campaign was entered upon Thursday, when it became apparent that the solons at Carson City were awaiting some manifestation of the sentiment prevailing in this city concerning the present law.

Some of the legislators have felt that the people of Reno were lukewarm in the matter of amending the law to increase the residence period, and they notified local leaders of the

Nevada State Journal
February 1, 1913
Support organized by women was an influential consideration in a change to divorce law in 1913.

the 1950s.

Mentioned in an earlier chapter, the Nevada WCTU had an important reform agenda, and they lobbied in support of legal changes for several issues. In 1903 they supported increasing the fine for the sale of liquor to minors. During the 1909 legislative session Nevada WCTU members circulated a petition for a bill to raise the age of consent to eighteen for girls. The age had been lowered to fourteen in the previous session, and supporters of an increase succeeded in raising it to sixteen with this effort.

With their emphasis on legal safeguards for women, the Nevada WCTU reflected the interests and efforts of women in national reform movements. Prostitution, considered a tremendous social evil, was under attack throughout the nation. Vice investigations in large cities raised fears of white slavery, and there were sensationalized and lurid accounts of young girls kidnapped, drugged, and forced into prostitution and drug abuse. The Mann Act, a federal law prohibiting the transportation of women across state lines for immoral purposes, was passed in 1910. There was anti-vice activity in Nevada, too. In 1913 the legislature passed laws that made it illegal to advertise prostitution or to live off the earnings of a prostitute, and the WCTU had lobbied for a law against white slavery. In subsequent years, group members lobbied and supported laws to abolish prize fights, and gambling, and urged the creation of an industrial school for boys.

One issue that was significantly affected by women's political activism was the business of divorce in Nevada. In 1913 women campaigned vigorously to extend the residency requirement in Nevada from six months to one year, supporting passage of the Barnes Bill. The change would affect the lucrative legal and service sectors which did business with the outsiders who came to Nevada to obtain a divorce under the state's relatively lenient laws. By doubling the length of time required to establish the legal residency that entitled them to a divorce in the state, the new law would remove one of the attractive enticements to divorce in Nevada. The one year law would, and did, diminish divorce as business in Nevada, particularly in Reno, which attracted the bulk of the profitable trade. The destruction of the divorce industry was a part of general reform advocated by many church and club groups in the Progressive era, the first two decades of the twentieth century. Reformers feared that easy divorce would

WESTERN UNION TELEGRAM

NEWCOMB CARLTON, PRESIDENT

(5/)

CLASS OF SERVICE	SYMBOL
Day Message	
Day Letter	Blue
Night Message	Nite
Night Letter	N L

CLASS OF SERVICE	SYMBOL
Day Message	
Day Letter	Blue
Night Message	Nite
Night Letter	N L

RECEIVED AT

2 SFD 64-5EX NL

LAS VEGAS NEV 812PM MAR 24-17

HON E D BOYLE, GOV.

STATE BOARD OF EDUCATION, CARSON CITY NEV.

WE APPEAL TO YOU FOR LENIENCY IN CASE MISS BERTHA
JACKSON TEACHER IN OUR HIGH SCHOOL WHO FAILED IN TEACHERS
EXAMINATION IN DECEMBER SHE IS MOST EXCELLENT TEACHER AND TO
LOSE HER NOW WITH ONLY NINE WEEKS REMAINING WOULD MEAN GREAT
LOSS TO THE SCHOOL SHE EXPECTS ARIZONA CERTIFICATE SOON THE
PEOPLE OF LASVEGAS ENDORSE ME IN THIS

HELEN J STEWART,

CLERK COUNTY BOARD OF EDUCATION

840AM

Las Vegas, Nevada
May 22, 1917

The Honorable Emmet D. Boyle
Governor of Nevada,
Carson City, Nevada

GOVERNOR'S OFFICE
MAY 25 1917
Answered May 27

My dear Sir:

Last September the
State Board of Education granted
me a provisional certificate
until the December examination.
Since I failed to pass the examination, which pertained only to
the History and Methods of Education, will the State Board
accept in lieu of the examination credits in the required
subjects from an accredited

Requesting political favors often involved both men and women. In this case, Helen Stewart, a well known Las Vegas rancher, petitioned Governor Boyle for intervention with the Board of Education to allow Miss Bertha Jackson to continue teaching although she had not met all the requirements for certification. (Nevada State Library & Archives)

destroy the American family, which they perceived as an important foundation of American culture.

Mrs. George Bartlett was one of the women leading the grass roots movement to lengthen the residency requirement. Ironically, her husband later became famous nationwide as a Nevada divorce judge. In 1913, however, Mrs. Bartlett was a highly visible leader of the anti-divorce movement and told the *Nevada State Journal*, "Sentiment among the mothers in Reno is practically unanimous in favor of an amendment to the law." Women in Reno, prompted by members of the Twentieth Century Club, wrote letters to legislators, and circulated petitions supporting the change. A delegation of reformers, 160 according to the *Nevada State Journal*, traveled to Carson City on the Virginia & Truckee Railroad, and crowded into the legislative chambers to ensure passage of the law. The Barnes Bill passed 30 to 22.

Success with this issue was relatively fleeting. During the next legislative session, in 1915, the residency requirement was returned to six months. The political lobbying of Nevada women was no match for the traditional exchange of favors common in politics. Churchill County Senator Keddie wanted the State Fair moved to Fallon; border counties in the west wanted the divorce business back in Nevada. The legislators traded votes, and Reno divorce was back in business.

Women continued to lobby for issues important to them, and much of the organization to exert legislative influence came from women's clubs. In 1915 the magazine of the General Federation of Women's Clubs featured a legislative report by Bird Wilson, who was chairman of Nevada's Legislative Committee. She concluded that Nevada women didn't achieve all that they had hoped for, but important gains had been made: mother's pensions; a change in the inheritance law that benefitted women; a bill providing for kindergartens; and one regarding teachers's pensions.

Even after they gained the vote, women continued to use, as did men, political connections to further their agenda. In 1917, Helen Stewart, a Las Vegas pioneer and well connected Clark County resident, used her political clout and her position on the county Board of Education on behalf of a local teacher. Bertha Johnson had failed a certification examination, but the Board, impressed with her skills, requested that she be allowed to finish the term. Teachers were never abundant in the rural areas and small towns of Nevada and the situ-

Despite the political inroads made by Sadie Hurst and candidates like Anne Martin, it was much more common for women to enter the chambers of the legislature as clerical help. In this 1921 picture of the Elko delegation one of the women is identified as Miss A.C. Henderson, the committee clerk; the other women is unidentified. It is not clear which woman is Miss Henderson. (Nevada State Library & Archives)

ation had been exacerbated by the war, when many young male teachers went off to military service. The teacher shortage was probably a factor in the bid to keep Johnson's services. Whatever the motivation, the lobbying was successful and Governor Boyle sent a telegram supporting Johnson's case.

In the years after they gained the vote in Nevada in 1914, a number of women succeeded in their bids for elected office. Edna Catlin Baker was the first female to be elected to a statewide office when she filed for and won a position on the University's Board of Regents. Mary Bray solicited Governor Boyle for an appointment to a vacant position as a Washoe County Commissioner in 1916. Several women were on the ballot in the 1920 primary as candidates for presidential electors.

It was the assembly race for the third district in 1918, however, that was most significant for women. Sadie D. Hurst was listed as one of the candidates. Publicly and enthusiastically endorsed by women's groups, she became the first woman elected to the legislature in Nevada. A native of Iowa and a widow, Sadie Hurst came west to Reno with her adult sons. She was deeply involved in club work, and was president of the Washoe County Equal Franchise Society in 1914, and president of the Women's Citizen's Club in 1916.

After her election, Assemblywoman Hurst announced her intention to submit several bills, a number of which would deal with women's issues. Her first legislative request was a resolution regarding the women's suffrage amendment which was adopted. She also presented bills relating to the guardianship of minors, women's rights regarding community property, cruelty to animals, and several others. A complex woman, Hurst was publicly opposed to a bill that permitted marriage between Caucasians and Indians, which had long been illegal under Nevada law. She declared that she did not believe in the "intermingling" of races.

The Nineteenth Amendment altered the constitution and mandated that the right to vote could not be denied or abridged based on sex, and Nevada called a special legislative session in February 1920 to ratify that change. That session marked an important moment for women who had worked hard to secure the vote, and Hurst, as the first female legislator, occupied the Speaker's chair during the vote on the resolution. Hurst was at Governor Emmet Boyle's shoulder when he signed the resolution, and she spoke at the ratification cer-

Elko Daily Free Press, *December 11, 1918*

As the first woman elected to the Nevada Legislature, Mrs. Sadie Hurst was easily identifiable in the official portrait for the 1919 legislative session. (Nevada State Library & Archives)

In 1920 Governor Emmet Boyle signed the resolution ratifying the 19th Amendment to the U.S. Constitution, an event that marked the end of a long struggle. (Nevada Historical Society)

emony held in August of that year.

Sadie Hurst lost her bid for reelection in 1920, but continued with her club work until she moved to California in 1922. Her defeat, however, did not mark the end of women's success in the political arena, and many more women were elected to office in the coming decades. In *The Long Campaign*, Anne Bail Howard has chronicled the life and work of another woman who played a major role in Nevada politics and lost an important election that year. 1920 marked Anne Martin's second campaign for a seat in the U. S. Senate. Martin was born in one of Nevada's frontier towns. Empire was a rugged, bustling lumber camp near Carson City. Her father had started as a clerk in a store, but he invested wisely and became successful and financially comfortable. He was elected to the Nevada legislature in 1875, the same year Anne was born. The family moved to Reno in 1883, where Martin went into the mercantile business.

Anne Martin was a bright student, and attended Stanford University for undergraduate work and an M.A. in history. She returned to Reno in 1897 to teach history at the Nevada State University. She left the University in 1899, and went east, where she attended classes at Columbia, then traveled through Europe. Martin met Emmeline Pankhurst in London and worked with the women's suffrage effort in England. In 1910 she participated in a rush on the House of Commons, and was arrested along with 113 other women.

Inspired by the demonstrations and sacrifice that she witnessed, Martin returned to Nevada determined to win the vote for American women. She was president of the Nevada Equal Franchise Society, and an active and determined supporter of the suffrage movement. Once women gained the vote, Anne Martin launched an attempt to win a political office. In 1918, she was the first Nevada woman to run for the U.S. Senate. Losing in that election, she tried again in 1920, and was again defeated. She didn't see her defeats as failures, however; she believed that the votes she attracted were women voting for a woman, and important for that reason.

Martin's loss in the Senate races did not mark the end of her political and reform activity. She was a member of the Women's International League for Peace and Freedom, and was a delegate to the League's World Congresses: Dublin in 1926 and Prague in 1929. Even after she retired to Carmel, California, she embarked on a letter writing campaign to urge the president of Stanford to hire more

ANNE MARTIN

Lunico Cantidato pel Senato degli Stati Uniti che si impegna per il benessere del popolo.

Indipentente da qualunque partito interessato nei guadagni eccessivi dalle grande case commerciali e nella politica.

E in favore di avere il terreno Governativo nello Stato di Nevada diviso in mido tale da poterne usare ogni agricoltore individualmente beneficato.

Fara' ogni suo possibile onde dare il suo appoggio al Presidente come capo del popolo.

Crede fermamente essere questa una guerra del Popolo e che' possa alla discussione dei termini di pace l'interesse dei lavoratori sia ovunque e sopra ogni cosa salvaguardata.

ANNE MARTIN
IL CANTIDATO DEL POPOLO DEL
SENATO DEGLI STATI UNITI

Eleggete Anne Martin, Datele l'Opportunita' di Combattere Per Voi Nel Seneto.

Anne Martin ran for U. S. Senate in 1918 and 1920. Some of her campaign literature was aimed at the Italian-Americans in Nevada. (University of Nevada, Reno, Special Collections)

Upper left, Mary Rose
Mary Rose was the first female legislator from Humboldt County. Defeated in subsequent elections, she served only one term. She was appointed State Land Registrar by Governor Vail Pittman in 1934. (Humboldt County Museum)

Upper right, Daisy Allen
There were four women in the assembly in the 1925 session. Daisy Allen was a business woman from Churchill County. (Nevada State Library & Archives)

Left center, Bertha Knemeyer
Bertha Knemeyer, the daughter of German immigrants, was born in Carson City in 1885. After graduation from the University of Nevada in Reno, she began teaching high school in Elko in 1906. When she assumed the duties of Deputy Superintendent of Public instruction for northeastern Nevada at age thirty, she was the first woman appointed to that office. (Northeastern Nevada Museum)

Bottom, Luella Drum
A business woman from Churchill County, Luella Drum was elected to the Assembly for the 1939 session. (Nevada State Library & Archives)

Glenn Edna Grier was an Assemblywoman from White Pine County in 1935, then administered the women's division of the W.P.A. in Nevada. (Nevada State Library & Archives)

women faculty. Anne Martin died in Carmel in 1951.

Nevada women like Sadie Hurst and Anne Martin paved the way for political participation. Since Sadie Hurst's election to the Assembly in 1920, women have been a part of all but three Nevada legislatures, and their numbers have increased over the years. Women hold important and powerful offices in the legislative structure and by the 1995 session, women constituted one-third of the elected body.

In the 1930s Glenn Edna Grier was one of the women entering the political arena, both in an elected and an appointed capacity. A native of Ohio, Glenn Edna Park moved with her family to Kansas, where her father homesteaded on land granted to Civil War veterans. She passed the Kansas teacher's examination at age sixteen, then taught for several years. After she married, she moved with her husband to Provo, Utah, then to Ely, Nevada in 1911.

Mrs. Grier was widowed in 1930, retiring from a position with J. C. Penneys in 1933. With time on her hands, she ran for the Assembly in 1934 when she was sixty-six years old. Campaigning throughout White Pine County, she drove alone to isolated ranches, mines, and sheep camps. She won the election and went to Carson City for the 1935 legislative session. At the end of her first session, Senator Key Pittman appointed Grier administrator of the women's division of the WPA. For several years she traveled throughout the state in this capacity. She retired again when the project ended and returned to Ely.

Josie Alma Woods was a legislator from Eureka. A rancher, she decided to run for a seat on the County Commission in 1940, but received less than one quarter of the votes cast. In 1942, she again ran for office, this time seeking a position in the State Assembly. She succeeded, and along with Mary Sharp of Nye County, was a member of the 1943 legislature. She was re-elected in 1944, and in 1945 was one of three women in the Assembly. She failed to win a third term, unable to overcome post-wartime sentiment favoring a returned war veteran. Josie Woods learned the hard lessons of politics in her defeat. She had planned to run for the Senate in 1946, but ran for the Assembly again when the incumbent senator promised party political support. When she lost her bid for re-election, she believed that she had been the victim of a "political deal."

Women continued to wield political power behind the scenes. One of the most influential women among the power brokers in

STATE OF NEVADA

Assembly Concurrent Resolution No. 30

Introduced by deBraga, Hickey, Ohrenschall, Tiffany, Carpenter, Segerblom, Marvel, Neighbors, Berman, Williams, Buckley, Perkins, Arberry, Giunchigliani, Herrera, Close, Humke, Amodei, Von Tobel, Goldwater, Evans, Krenzer, Manendo, Nolan, Price, Sandoval, Mortenson, Cegavske, Collins, Chowning, Ernaut, Hettrick, Gustavson, Lee, Koivisto, Parks, Braunlin, Lambert, Freeman, Bache, Anderson and Dini

WHEREAS, The members of the Nevada Legislature were saddened to learn of the passing of pioneer rancher and former Assemblywoman Josie Alma Woods on February 19, 1983; and

WHEREAS, Josie Alma Woods was born in Clyde, Texas, on December 29, 1889; and   WHEREAS, Arriving in Nevada in the early 1900's, Josie Alma Woods spent 5 years riding a circuit between mining towns in a buckboard, assisting business partner, Dr. Mabel Young, in her dentistry practice; and

WHEREAS, In 1915, they purchased a 1911 Model T and, because it had a tendency to break down, they paid a mechanic $25 to take the engine apart, describe the works and show them how to repair it themselves; and

WHEREAS, Josie Alma Woods purchased 40 head of cattle at an estate auction and acquired a former stagecoach and Pony Express station located between Eureka and Austin, Nevada, which she named "The Willows"; and

WHEREAS, Josie Alma Woods, with no previous ranching experience, soon became known as an expert judge of cattle and transformed the 320-acre homestead into a successful cattle ranch, encompassing 1,200 square miles by the time it was sold in 1954; and

WHEREAS, In 1942, Josie Alma Woods was the first woman elected to the Nevada Legislature as a representative of Eureka County and, in 1944, she was reelected, serving two terms in the Nevada State Assembly; and

WHEREAS, Josie Alma Woods was the first woman appointed to serve on the Assembly Standing Committee on Taxation and the Assembly Standing Committee on Banks and Banking; and

WHEREAS, Josie Alma Woods was a member of the Eureka County Farm Bureau, the Eureka Business and Professional Women's Club, and the National and State Livestock Associations; and

WHEREAS, Josie Alma Woods embodied the true spirit of the pioneer woman, so much so that her life story was the basis for the popular movie "The Ballad of Josie," which starred Doris Day; now, therefore, be it

RESOLVED BY THE ASSEMBLY OF THE STATE OF NEVADA, THE SENATE CONCURRING, That the members of the 69th session of the Nevada Legislature extend their belated and sincere condolences to the family and friends of Josie Alma Woods; and be it further

RESOLVED, That the Nevada Legislature celebrates the life and legacy of a pioneer woman who personified the contributions that women have made in our state; and be it further

RESOLVED, That the Chief Clerk of the Assembly prepare and transmit a copy of this resolution to the nieces and nephews of Josie Alma Woods: Mary June Bell, Douglas Woods, Robert Odle, Edward Odle and Kenneth Phillips.

ADOPTED BY THE ASSEMBLY
May 28, 1997

Joseph E. Dini, Jr.
Speaker of the Assembly

Linda B. Alden
Chief Clerk of the Assembly

ADOPTED BY THE SENATE
May 28, 1997

Lawrence E. Jacobsen
President Pro Tempore of the Senate

Janice L. Thomas
Secretary of the Senate

Recognition of the political and personal achievement of women is sometimes belated. Josie Woods, an Assemblywoman from Eureka in 1942, was honored in State of Nevada Assembly Concurrent Resolution No. 30 in 1997. (Assembly, State of Nevada)

Washington and Nevada was Eva Adams. Born in Wonder, Nevada, in 1908 Adams moved around with her family and grew up in mining camps. Her father operated hotels in Fairview, Aurora, Buckthorn, and Thompson. She was a 1928 graduate of the University of Nevada, and went on to Columbia University for an M.A. in English in 1936. She continued her education while working and earned a law degree from American University in 1950, then a master's in law from George Washington University.

In 1940 Adams became administrative assistant for Senator Patrick McCarran of Nevada. Much as Hannah Clapp had done for Senator Stewart, she kept Senator McCarran informed of local happenings while he was in Washington. In a letter to McCarran in the fall of 1940, Adams relates social happenings and gossip but also indicates that she is working, "I'm going to Carson Saturday - if all goes well - and pay `official visits' on the people I think you would want me to see. Tomorrow night I'm going to the Big Rally here in the State Building, to hear Pittman and Scrugham. Al Cahlan is coming in tonight." She concludes with the reminder, "If you want information you aren't getting, you have only to say the word, as you know...."[ellipses in original].

Senator McCarran died while campaigning in 1954 and Eva Adams continued her position as assistant under Ernest Brown, who was appointed by Governor Russell to fill McCarran's position, then under Alan Bible, who won the election to the position in 1954. In 1961 Eva received her own political position when President Kennedy appointed her Director of the U. S. Mint. There was talk of a bid for governor in 1970 but no candidacy resulted.

In a newspaper interview just after her appointment to the Mint, Adams was asked about her advice to young women interested in a career in government. She believed that women did indeed belong in government but it took hard work, "you can't get there except by getting in and plodding." She recommended involvement in a political club and a college major of political science. She also advised that women retain their femininity, "You can be appealing looking and soft-voiced without being weak." Her views are a revealing reflection of her time. It was difficult for women, who were definitely in the minority, to work with men as equals.

Nevada women had overcome a number of barriers as they emerged into public life. As club women and temperance supporters

Possibly one of the most important women in Nevada politics, Eva Adams worked with some of Nevada's most powerful men in Washington, and was appointed Director of the U.S. Mint. (University of Nevada, Reno, Special Collections)

African-American women exerted political power when they participated in demonstrations supporting basic civil rights. (University of Nevada, Reno, Special Collections)

they worked for better communities. As suffrage supporters and political women they worked to improve their own condition and that of the state in general. And as working women they — worked. As in these other arenas, however, there were obstacles to be overcome in Nevada women's self-determination in job and career.

WOMEN OF NEVADA

Patronize Home Industry *if* Gold Medal and Riverside Flour
A Duty and a Pleasure *if* Gold Medal and Sagebrush Crackers

THE BRIDE'S FIRST LOAF

RIVERSIDE MILL COMPANY
ESTABLISHED 1889

RENO   CAPITAL AND SURPLUS, $250,000.00   NEVADA

As illustrated by this 1912 advertisement for the Riverside Mill Company, and the designation as the "bride's first loaf," the ideal place for a woman was believed to be in the home, working for the care and comfort of her husband and family, and taking pride in her housekeeping skills. (Nevada Historical Society)

NEVADA WOMEN IN THE WORK FORCE

An important aspect of the emergence of American women from the domestic sphere into the public arena was work for pay outside the home. Women, of course, have worked domestically and publicly from earliest periods of American settlement and from the earliest periods of settlement in Nevada. The number of women working for wages and the type of work done by women outside the home, however, has altered significantly, particularly in the twentieth century. Women have become more visible in the public sphere of the paid work force.

The middle-class ideal for women was that of wife, mother, and homemaker; the smiling young woman proudly displaying the "bride's first loaf" personifies that ideal. The advertisement probably is, in fact, a generally accurate representation of the satisfaction and joy that a new wife of the middle class would have taken in the tangible evidence of her domestic skills. The light and even texture of a perfectly browned loaf was proof that she had succeeded in her work as a wife, and fulfilled her own expectations was well as those of husband, family and neighbors. But domestic labor was only one kind of "women's work."

The activities documented in previous chapters indicate that there were many women in Nevada who had the means and the opportunity to devote themselves to charitable and political activities without the necessity of earning a living for themselves or contributing to the family income. While it is true that some of the women associated with club work, temperance, suffrage, and political activities were also working for money outside the home, the majority of women devoting themselves to worthy causes were middle-class homemakers, engaging in another kind of "women's work." Women were working hard on club activities and for the temperance and suffrage causes, but generally not for a salary.

D

DANGBERY, FREDERICK, farmer, res Third bet. Nevada and
    Division
David Henry, carpenter, with H. Meyer
Davies W. W., attorney at law, res Minnesota
DAVIS, E. A., dealer in Stoves and Tinware, Carson
Davis, Ephraim, boot-maker, Carson
DAVIS, GEORGE T., General Merchandise, Carson
Davis Miss Phoebe, seamstress
Dealy James E., bar-keeper, with G. Lewis
DEASON, S. C., District Attorney, and Attorney at Law
Doly Merechal, saloon, Carson
Donnelly Bernard, cook
Doran Louis, clerk, State library

Carson City directory, 1863
*The reality of family life in early Nevada, versus the middle-class ideal, was that
both married and single women worked outside the home. According to the city
directory, Miss Phoebe Davis was employed as a seamstress in Carson City in
1863. (Nevada State Library & Archives)*

APPLICANTS ARE MANY AT ELKO LAND OFFICE

Miss Fern Woodgate has accepted a position as cashier at the New Golden Rule Store.

During the first ten days of November, the United States land office in Elko has done a land office business in the strictest application of the term. New entries and final proofs are as follows:

ELKO AND LAMOILLE ON ITINERARY OF 6 WEEKS' TOUR TO TEACH WOMEN

*Newspapers of the early 20th century list a variety of occupations for women.
Some were typical, such as store cashier, home economics teacher, or dance
instructor; others were more unusual, as illustrated by the notice of the lady
assistant in the funeral home and the women filing for homestead in Elko
county. One advertisement promoted hairdressing as, "The best paying
profession for Women and Girls." (Nevada State Library & Archives)*

In addition to the unpaid labor that women performed, there were numerous types of jobs that women worked to earn money. Paid working women spanned the labor spectrum, from unskilled drudgery to careers as highly trained professional women. Single and married women worked to contribute to the family income; widowed, divorced, and abandoned women worked to support themselves and their families; single and, to a lesser extent, married women pursued education and careers. The careers of some women who worked for pay have been well documented. The life paths, that of a career or work for pay, pursued by female physicians Elizabeth Blackwell and Mary Putnam Jacobi and writers Catharine Maria Sedgwick and Louisa May Alcott, have been well documented. Other women worked anonymously as domestics in the homes of middle-class and wealthy Americans; native-born and immigrant women took in piece work and sewed long hours in crowded tenement quarters; and some labored in the factories in Lowell, Massachusetts, and other cities across the nation. Elizabeth Murray, a Boston businesswoman of the mid-eighteenth century who acquired assets of her own and protected them with a pre-nuptial agreement, was unique for her time. But over the course of two centuries increasing numbers of American women were unable or unwilling to attempt to live the domestic ideal as they sought fair wages for their skills and labor.

From the earliest settlement period women in Nevada also worked for pay outside the home. The majority of Euro-American women working for wages were young and single, and assumed domestic duties within the home after marriage. Most women who worked outside the home in the nineteenth century and well into the twentieth, labored in occupations that were considered acceptable for women, employment that was, broadly, an expansion of domestic duties within the home. There were, of course, exceptions and women's jobs could be as diverse as the women themselves. There is a wealth of material to be examined, and lives and activities yet to be recognized and understood. A number of scholars, however, have made important beginnings.

Comstock Women: The Making of a Mining Community, edited by Ronald M. James and C. Elizabeth Raymond, documents the diversity of women's work in Nevada's most famous nineteenth century mining locale. In Virginia City and the surrounding towns, women supported themselves and their families by running lodging houses,

Newspapers of the early 20th century

by using their needlework skills, and by telling fortunes or by communicating with those who had passed over. And some, although not as many as historical myth asserts, engaged in less respectable types of commerce, exchanging companionship and sex for cash.

Julie Nicoletta notes in her chapter in *Comstock Women*, "Redefining Domesticity: Women and Lodging Houses on the Comstock," that most women who kept house for pay were not married; they tended to be never-married, widowed or divorced. Margaret Fraser continued to run the Comstock House in Virginia City for two decades after divorcing her husband. Rose Conners was a widow who operated another Virginia City lodging house business. Some women who took in boarders, however, were married. Their lodgers shared the home with a husband and children. Amelia Steele employed servants and cooks in the lodging house where she resided with her husband and fifteen boarders. The paid work of women of color and of various ethnicities can be difficult to pinpoint, but Nicoletta has documented Chu Suh and Gee Pan, two single Chinese women, who operated a boarding house in 1880.

Mary McNair Mathews, whose activities mentioned in earlier chapters illustrate so many aspects of Nevada women in the public domain, worked at a variety of jobs for pay to support herself and her young son while she lived in Virginia City. Mathews took obvious pride in her willingness and ability to do whatever was necessary to earn money. She took in sewing and laundry, wrote letters for a fee, babysat, sat with the sick at night, took in boarders, and conducted her own school for more than a year. Her book, *Ten Years in Nevada*, is sprinkled with notations about the money she earned for many of these endeavors, as well as comments on her careful money management.

Mathews described the long days she worked while she was doing laundry, sewing, and conducting her school simultaneously. She rose early to do wash, taught between nine and noon, then spent her leisure time sewing over the lunch break and in the evening after she had finished supper. On Tuesdays she starched clothes at noon, and ironed them after school and in the evening. She was, indeed, an energetic woman. The hard work took its toll, and Mathews ended her laundry business when she determined it was "breaking her down." The monotonous and arduous toil undertaken by Mathews could be typical of the work for wages performed by women.

Some women's work outside the home was very much in the public spotlight, as was the case with opera singer Emma Nevada. (Nevada Historical Society)

The work associated with housekeeping in the nineteenth century, and earlier periods, could, indeed, "break" a woman down. Domestic labor, both private and paid, did not end when the sun went down or the clock struck six. Women's work continued, hour after hour, season after season. That sustained and intense labor changed as industrialization lightened the workload for women in the nineteenth century. Items such as purchased cloth, soap, and lamp oil made house keeping a bit easier. The work was still hard, however, for women who carried water (and waste), stoked heating and cooking stoves, preserved and prepared food, sewed family clothing, and spent hours laboring over washtubs and ironing boards. In the twentieth century, the advent of many more manufactured goods, as well as amenities like piped household water, electricity, and gas for lighting and heating eased the load even more.

The automobile facilitated women's duties, although twentieth-century women found that transportation responsibilities absorbed increasing amounts of their time, a reality documented by historian Virginia Scharff in *Taking the Wheel*. Despite the encroachments on women's time, the auto allowed many women access to jobs and work for pay. In 1915, Nevada dentist Mabel Young purchased a 1911 Model T for use in her rural dental practice.

Many of the goods and labor-saving technologies developed in the nineteenth and twentieth centuries were not readily available to all women. Poorer people and those in rural areas either could not afford or did not have access to modern conveniences, and women in those circumstances continued the heavy labor of the past. Reno had electric streetlights by 1887, but electrification was slower to come in the sparsely populated expanses of the state. In the rural area of Lund, Nevada, in White Pine County, a few individual households used generators by the 1930s to provide electricity. Only in 1939 did a large diesel generator furnish electricity to many of the homes in town.

It was not the norm, but there was glamorous and lucrative work for women. The working life of an entertainer, making beautiful music and bowing before an appreciative audience, was a stark contrast to the clank of a hand-operated washer and the generally unappreciative audience of small children. Emma Wixom Nevada was one of Nevada's celebrated working women. The daughter of a physician, Wixom was born in Nevada City, California, and moved to

Among the first female physicians to practice in Nevada, Dr. Eliza Cook chose a non-traditional career path. The nurturing aspect of her career, considered a female trait, is clear in this photograph. (Carson Valley Museum)

Austin, Nevada in 1863, as a small child. She received some voice training there, and her singing was popular with locals. Wixom was a talented linguist who learned to sign for the deaf, and spoke Washoe, Paiute, and Shoshone. She returned to California to attend Mills College in Oakland, where she studied German, Italian, French, and Spanish. She had planned to teach German at Mills, but was persuaded to pursue further musical training in Europe.

Her stage name, Emma Nevada, was chosen for her first concert in 1879, based on her connection with Nevada City as well as the state of Nevada. She was very successful, and toured both the United States and Europe several times. After her San Francisco performance in 1885, newspapers reported that the crowds expressed "enthusiasm bordering on lunacy." She encountered similar fervor on her return to Nevada, where she sang in Piper's Opera house in Virginia City, and in her home town of Austin.

Emma Nevada married an English physician who became her manager, and eventually retired to England. She trained her daughter Mignon, who also had a successful career. Wixom died in England in 1940. With wild adulation for her performances throughout the U.S. and before European royalty, Emma Nevada not a typical working women but definitely stepped beyond the bounds of the domestic sphere. Other women used different talents and skills to move beyond the limitations often imposed on women in the nineteenth and early twentieth centuries.

Dr. Eliza Cook was an early female physician (she wrote in her memoirs that she was the first woman to practice in Nevada) who expanded the caretaking role deemed natural for women into a career and work for pay. She was born in 1856 in Salt Lake City, Utah, and moved to the Carson Valley in 1870 with her mother and sister. Interested in medicine as a girl, Cook worked with a physician in Genoa, Dr. W. H. Smith. Dr. Smith encouraged her to pursue medicine, and she studied with him to prepare for college. She graduated from Cooper Medical College, now Stanford University, in 1884, then went on to the Women's Medical College of Philadelphia, and post graduate work in New York. She returned to Carson Valley and, by the early 1890s, had established a medical practice, where she worked for more than forty years. As with housework, working as a physician was a physically strenuous job. Dr. Cook traveled around the valley in a horse and buggy to care for her patients, which added

Women were making some headway as professionals near the end of the 19th century. Dr. Helen Rulison Shipley practiced dentistry in this ornate Victorian office. (Nevada State Museum)

Myrtle Granger Pulsipher
Expanding cooking and housekeeping chores into the public realm were natural extensions of the domestic sphere, and an acceptable choice for women working outside the home. (Desert Valley Museum)

to the long hours spent with laboring mothers, ailing children, and injured farm hands. She later took advantage of modern technology and made her rounds in a model T. Cook never married, but she kept her own home and cooked and cleaned for herself.

Eliza Cook was one of the working women who did find time to become involved in community and reform activities. She was active in the suffrage movement, and was a vice president of the Nevada Equal Suffrage Association, 1895-1896. She had rejected the idea of a man's dominance over woman when she read as a young girl the biblical command that man should rule over woman. She was also a member of the Nevada WCTU, and served that organization as president from 1896 to 1901. Certainly as a physician, she would have been aware of the domestic disruption and health problems associated with alcoholism. Concerned with political issues, she wrote letters to express her opinions to Nevada congressmen. Eliza Cook apparently thrived on hard work, and was healthy and active until her death at ninety-one.

Helen Rulison, who was born in Dayton, Nevada in 1870, also pursued a non-traditional career path, but only after first doing "women's work." An 1889 graduate of the University of Nevada, Rulison taught in Reno for several years then went back to school at the University of California in San Francisco. She completed a course in dentistry, and practiced in San Francisco until moving to Goldfield in 1907, becoming the only female dentist in that booming mining center. She moved on to Tonopah in 1912. There she met Robert Shipley, and the couple married just before her forty-sixth birthday, in 1916. Dr. Shipley continued to practice dentistry in Tonopah, and later Reno, where she moved in 1926. She retired in 1946, just nine years before her death in 1955 at age eighty-four.

Work as a physician or dentist were only two of many occupations traditionally reserved for men that women in Nevada pursued. The federal Homestead Acts of 1860 and 1890 provided land for men and women who could fulfill the residency and improvement requirements. Women most often homesteaded with a family, but some women did homestead on their own. It's not clear under what circumstances Lizzie Smith and Elizabeth Wieland filed Homestead Application and Desert Homestead Final Proof, respectively, in Elko County in 1914. Women frequently filed for land adjacent to family homesteads, but they were legally entitled to land for their own use.

Department of Public Instruction

State of ⟨seal⟩ Nevada

This Certifies, That *Stella Champo*, a Pupil in the Public School of *Las Vegas* District, County of *Clark*, has completed and satisfactorily passed examination in the Course of Study prescribed by the State Board of Education for the Grammar Department of the Public Schools of this State; and, in consideration thereof, and of *her* studious habits and good character, *she* is granted this

Certificate of Promotion

Entitling *her* to enter any High School in the State of Nevada.

Given at *Las Vegas*, Nevada, this *25th* day of *May*, A.D. 192*7*.

W. J. Hunting
State Superintendent of Public Instruction.

Eva M. Wilson
Teacher.

Maude Frazier
Deputy Superintendent District No. *5*.

It was the middle-class ideal for wives and mothers to stay at home, but for working class and immigrant women work outside the home had long been a reality. Stella Champo came to the U.S. from Italy as an infant. Her family settled in Las Vegas in 1912. She worked for many years as a waitress, cashier, and hostess. (Special Collections, University of Nevada, Las Vegas)

Women did own and work ranches and farms in Nevada, acquiring land through homestead, or by purchasing a farm or ranch outright. Some inherited property from a father or husband, as was the case with Helen Wiser Stewart, who ran a large southern Nevada ranching operation after her husband's death.

Helen Stewart came to Nevada from Sacramento in 1873 after her marriage. Her husband, Archibald Stewart, operated a successful freighting business in Pioche, then purchased a ranch in the Las Vegas valley. In 1884, Stewart's husband was murdered by a hand on a neighboring ranch. She took over management of the Stewart ranch, and continued to raise their five children. With the help of Anglo and Native American ranch hands, she worked cattle, and raised and harvested fruit on the ranch. Stewart became the largest landowner in what was then Lincoln County, with over two thousand acres. When she married Frank Stewart, one of her ranch hands, in 1900, Helen Stewart contracted a prenuptial agreement to protect her property. When her first husband died intestate, she had faced the possibility of loss of the ranch and learned a hard lesson about women's property rights.

Other Nevada women worked the land successfully. Josie Alma Woods, who was also an assemblywoman from Eureka, started with a small piece of property, once a stagecoach and Pony Express Station. Woods transformed it into a thriving cattle ranch, and acquired a reputation, in the competitive male domain of ranching, as an excellent judge of livestock. When she sold her ranch in 1954 she owned over 1,200 square miles. In her early years in Nevada, Josie Woods traveled around the countryside in a buckboard with Dr. Mabel Young, assisting Dr. Young in her dental practice.

The lives and adventures of women property owners like Helen Stewart and Josie Alma Woods were extraordinary. They moved beyond the domestic sphere by going into business for themselves, providing for their own support, and with the case of Helen Stewart, support for a family. The ownership of their own property sets Stewart, Woods, and other business owners like them somewhat apart from other women who worked for wages. Nonetheless, if their profits weren't precisely wages, they were working outside the traditional women's domestic domain, and providing for themselves and their families.

Most women who supported themselves or worked for pay la-

This 1927 letter of recommendation reveals women working in the mercantile business, one as the employee, one as the business owner. (University of Nevada Las Vegas Special Collections)

The Mesquite school had both two male teachers and one female teacher in 1914. (Desert Valley Museum)

bored in jobs that were more mainstream, those that were considered appropriate for women at the time. As they had done on the Comstock in the nineteenth century, women in the twentieth century continued to perform domestic tasks for pay. Granger's cafe and boarding house, in the southern Nevada town of Mesquite, with the tasks of cooking and cleaning, clearly fell within the traditional boundaries of domestic duties for women. A basic education prepared women for a variety of jobs considered appropriate for females. Stella Champo, with a high school diploma, worked most of her life as a restaurant waitress or hostess.

With training or advanced education, there were other professions that also tapped into talents perceived as natural for women. By the early twentieth century a feminization of professions associated with nurturing or with a service orientation was apparent. Fields such as social work, teaching, library work, and nursing were dominated by women. Women in Nevada reflected these national trends in the occupations they pursued.

Although teaching was one of the professions that employed growing numbers of women, it has long been an acceptable and available career for women who wanted or needed to work. Beginning with the dame schools operated in colonial America, women have been working in the classroom. Early teachers needed only to know more than their students to be able to teach, and many were not much older than some of the young people they instructed. In the decades before and after the Civil War in America, many single women moved west and south, as frontier areas recruited for their schools. A school was beneficial to new communities. It was necessary, of course, to provide a basic education for children, but it was equally important to have a school as a symbol of stability and respectability in order to attract new settlers to the area. That was the case in both the old West, frontier areas in the Midwest and the Southeast, and the far west frontiers that became known as the new West. The movement south continued in the years after the Civil War as many women migrated to the South to found schools and teach the newly freed slaves.

As professional activities expanded in the schools, teachers and administrators organized to standardize the requirements for their type of work, and to bring respect and higher pay to their specialty. School districts also began to require certain levels of education or

Questions for the Examination of Teachers,

PREPARED BY THE

STATE BOARD OF EDUCATION.----JULY, 1894.

HISTORY UNITED STATES.

First and Second Grades.]   [Time, 90 minutes.

1. Give three reasons why one should have a good knowledge of the history of his country.

2. How was Texas acquired by the United States?

3. What were the principal charges against England in the Declaration of Independance? Name at least six.

4. Give a list of the more important political parties which have existed in the United States since the signing of the Declaration of Independence, and give some leading principles and purposes of each party.

5. Name six distinguished American statesmen, and give the leading idea which each represented.

6. (*a*) Name the original 13 States.

(*b*) Name three of the most revered men in our national history; three the most despised.

7. What American was most prominently associated with each of the following enterprises and inventions:

(*a*) The first steamboat on the Hudson; (*b*) the Erie canal; (*c*) the electric telegraph; (*d*) the reaper; (*e*) the sewing machine; (*f*) vulcanized rubber; (*g*) the Atlantic cable; (*h*) the electric light; (*i*) the cotton gin; (*j*) the monitor.

8. To what colonies did each of the following persons respectively belong: (*a*) Miles Standish; (*b*) Roger Williams; (*c*) John Smith; (*d*) Peter Stuyvesant; (*e*) James Oglethorpe?

Give two causes which led to the war of 1812.

9. (*a*) Name four distinguished Generals who became Presidents of the United States.

(*b*) How many men have served the nation as Presidents?

10. What political parties were formed at the close of the Revolutionary war, and what principles did each represent?

Teacher Examination Questions
Teaching was an acceptable working environment for women, although it was often limited to single women. (University of Nevada Las Vegas Special Collections)

skills of the teachers they hired. The offices of territorial superintendent of public instruction and county superintendent of county schools had been created by the Nevada Territorial Legislature. The law required that ten percent of the revenues from property taxes be set aside to hire and pay teachers. Certain monies from fines were also allocated for educational support.

In his *History of Nevada*, historian Russell Elliott noted that money for the support of schools was affected by the mining depression of 1880, and the declining population in the state. Local governments found it difficult to provide for the educational needs of children in their domain. Private schools, such as the Sierra Seminary operated by Hannah Clapp in Carson City, attempted to fill the gaps. Native-American children faced even greater obstacles to an education. Sarah Winnemucca, in addition to her political advocacy, operated a school for Paiute children in Lovelock.

Even working with limited funds, Nevada school districts were demanding basic levels of competency in the teachers they hired. In 1894 the Nevada State Board of Education administered qualifying examinations for teachers. Charles Thompson of Pioche took the test with one other man and two women. He saved his exam and recorded the scores on his copy; Mary Syphus and Annie Ronnow of Panaca both received higher scores. The scores of the men, however, were apparently high enough to pass. Teaching offered women, and, in smaller numbers men, a respectable career, and passing the exam was a significant achievement. Improving teacher competency was an ongoing effort by local school districts.

In 1907, spurred by the enthusiasm of early Progressive reform, a legislative Reorganization Act addressed the problems of schools. The State Board of Education was given more power, and standards for teachers were raised. The curriculum was also revamped and more centralization improved rural schools. By the mid-twentieth century school administrations in Nevada benefitted when more money was allotted for education to meet the needs of the rising numbers of school children in the decade after the Second World War.

Biennial reports filed by the Nevada Superintendent of Public Instruction, along with reports of many other state agencies, are printed in the Appendices to the Journals of the Senate and the Assembly. Individual reports of the deputy district superintendents are

THE TEACHERS

I cannot close without paying a tribute to the loyal teachers who have made possible the enviable reputation held by Nevada's schools. With many of them the work for the schools is, as it is with me, a real labor of love and when labor is thus dignified by the loftiest sentiment, real and lasting progress is attained. So I feel that Nevada owes a debt to her teachers that should be paid in part by salaries more nearly adequate to the service rendered and also by a just and cordial recognition of the great service given so freely and lovingly by them. Whether this work has been in book lines, in vocational lines or in war work and patriotism it has shown resplendent in the faces and lives of their pupils, and it will forever rank the teachers among the foremost of our country's civic patriots.

School Superintendent Report
The statistics in the Reports of District Superintendents for 1917-1918 for Elko County show that of the 114 teachers in the districts in 1918, 100 were women. The Deputy State Superintendent who filed the report was a woman, Bertha Knemeyer. (Nevada State Library & Archives)

included. In 1917 and 1918 Bertha Knemeyer was deputy for the First District in Elko County, the first woman appointed to that office. Her report provides a great deal of statistical information about schooling in Elko County for those years. The district was growing, and teachers salaries increased over the biennium, but there was a noticeable disparity in salaries between men and women. Women teachers averaged $95.50 per month for elementary teaching; there was no salary listing for male teachers in these grade levels. In the high schools, women averaged $137 each month, men were paid $175 per month. For principals, the differences were even greater: women principals received $135, men $211. Male high school teachers received a significantly higher salary than female principals.

Apparently the gap was narrowing; Superintendent Knemeyer reported that men had received an average 10.2% increase, and women had received a 12.7% increase since 1915. The school districts weren't necessarily exhausting their monies on the higher salaries for men by hiring large numbers of male teachers. Nevada reflected the national dominance of the teaching profession by women, and the lower paid women teachers far outnumbered men: 88 to 15 in 1917, 100 to 14 in 1918. John Bray was Superintendent of Public Instruction during 1917-1918. He commended the teachers for their fine work, commenting, "With many of them the work for the schools is, as it is with me, a real labor of love and when labor is thus dignified by the loftiest sentiment, real and lasting progress is attained." He went on to recommend such dedication be rewarded with salary increases. Salary equity was not mentioned in his suggestions, and the lower wages paid to women were not discussed in his report. At the time higher salaries for men were commonly justified with the assertion that men, as the head of a household, needed more money to support a family. Female teachers, and women workers in general, were single women responsible only for themselves. They often remained in the family home, or, in the case of teachers, were boarded with local families as a part of their salary, and thus could live on a lower income—or so common wisdom maintained. The reality, of course, often differed dramatically from perception, and working women in Nevada and elsewhere suffered with low wages.

A few working women in Nevada pursued teaching and education on an advanced level. Jeanne Elizabeth Weir was born in Iowa, and graduated from Iowa State Teacher's College in 1893. She taught

A professor of history and department chair at the University of Nevada in Reno and later director of the Nevada Historical Society, Jeanne Elizabeth Weir, expanded the traditional role of woman as teacher. (Nevada Historical Society)

Nursing was another career considered a natural choice for women to pursue. This is a scene from the 1920s or 30s. (University of Nevada, Reno, Special Collections)

Mary Virginia Perkins Lytle's medical career was a more traditional female role. She trained as a midwife to serve the women in the isolated town of Overton where she had been born and where she spent most of her life. (University of Nevada Las Vegas Special Collections)

in Iowa and Oregon, then came to Nevada. She returned to school and earned a B.A. from Stanford University and became professor of history, later department chair at the University of Nevada. Weir was one of the many Nevada women who worked and volunteered for a variety of projects and causes. She was a founder, in 1904, and director for many years of the Nevada Historical Society and a leader in the Nevada suffrage campaign. Jeanne Weir took a traditional women's field, teaching, a step further.

Nursing the sick was a responsibility that traditionally fell to women in the home, but as a paid profession was dominated by men. It was only as a result of women's nursing responsibilities during the Civil War that nursing became a respectable profession open to women, and, like teaching, it was a profession that came to be dominated by women in the twentieth century. The first American nursing school was opened in 1873, but many of the women who worked as nurses in the nineteenth and early twentieth centuries had little or no formal training. Very often they worked with a physician and were trained on the job, the same way many physicians had been trained throughout the nineteenth century. In Nevada, formal nurse's training was first established at St. Mary's Hospital in Reno, which graduated forty-eight nurses from their program in the years between 1912 and 1922.

Mary Virginia Perkins Lytle was a Nevada woman who pursued an education in the nursing profession to fill the needs in her own community. Born in Overton, Nevada in 1883, the daughter of Mormon settlers, she married John Lytle in 1904. After losing her first three daughters, Lytle realized that the shortage of medical personnel in Overton, which was small and isolated, could have tragic consequences. She trained as a nurse/midwife in 1908 in Salt Lake City and was certified by the Utah Medical Board in that year. Mary Lytle returned to Overton, where she had six more children and served as midwife for thirty-one years, delivering almost two hundred babies.

Midwives did practice in cities; Virginia City had at least one midwife listed in the 1862 city directory. The need was particularly critical, however, in isolated rural areas. Mary Oxborrow, a Mormon plural wife who emigrated to St. George, Utah from England as a young girl, moved to Lund, in White Pine County around 1899 as a widow with children. She, too, received training in Salt Lake City,

Native American women also worked outside the home. Washoe basketmaker Dat-So-La-Lee achieved fame with her artistry in her craft.
(Nevada Historical Society)

Growing up in a period of tremendous change, Wuzzie George passed on the traditional work of the women of her tribe, the Northern Paiutes near Stillwater, Nevada.
(Special Collections Department, University of Nevada, Reno, Margaret M. Wheat Collection)

then returned to Lund. Oxborrow provided medical care for the community, and delivered many babies until her death in 1935.

Immigrant women, native women, and women of color also worked in this most traditional of occupations for women. Florentina Manuella Mesa (Nellie) Nostrossa was a native of Peru who immigrated to California in 1848. She moved to Eureka, Nevada with her two children after her marriage ended. She received informal training by working as an assistant for local doctors. Midwifery was a common, highly valued, and very necessary skill and occupation, especially in rural Nevada. The importance of their work conferred status on these working women. Other women who worked for pay labored in jobs traditional for other cultures, and their work and cultural expectations could differ significantly from those of Euro-American culture.

Dat-So-La-Lee was a Native American women, a member of the tribe that had traditionally occupied territory in the Carson Valley and Alpine County, California. A skilled basket maker, she became famous for her degikup baskets, a circular basket that is woven into a distinctive shape with an expanded middle, having the base of the basket and the top opening of equal dimensions. The date of her birth is unknown, but was probably sometime around 1850. Her family lived in the Carson Valley, and Dat-So-La-Lee, also known as Louisa Keyser, cooked and laundered for miners, a common occupation for native women after Euro-American settlement. She worked for a family in Alpine County, California, and by 1895 was making baskets to sell. A Carson City merchant, Abe Cohn, sold her baskets in his emporium and became her sponsor.

Women of the Washoe tribe had been weaving baskets for thousands of years. Important tools for native groups who survived by hunting and gathering, the baskets were used for storage and transport. They were commonly constructed with a single-rod coiling technique, and very tightly woven with tiny stitches. A time consuming part of the work entailed gathering and drying the materials used in the baskets. Dat-So-La-Lee and her third husband, Charlie Keyser, were supported by the Cohns in exchange for the beautifully crafted baskets. Cohn actively promoted Dat-So-La-Lee's baskets and they commanded top prices. She wove baskets for Abe Cohn for thirty years, from 1895 until her death in 1925.

Wuzzie George was a Native American woman whose family life

Zilpha Hughes Guearo followed family tradition when she followed her father as postmaster of Mesquite in the early 20th century. (Desert Valley Museum)

Fannie Hazlett was appointed postmaster of Dayton in 1895. Hazlett, who had come overland to Nevada in 1862, took her first airplane ride at age 84. (Nevada Historical Society)

and working conditions highlight the changes wrought by the presence of Euro-American settlers in Nevada. Born in the early 1880s, George was Northern Paiute, and lived in the Stillwater area. As a small child she spent time with her grandmother while her mother washed dishes at a hotel. George and her grandmother also worked for pay, gathering wood for the hotel and receiving breakfast as payment. She also worked for a ranch family as a child.

Her grandmother's influence and training were important in helping Wuzzie George maintain the traditions of her tribe, particularly the work done by women. From her grandmother, as a child and as a young woman, she learned the basketmaking and food gathering techniques that had insured the survival of families in a harsh environment for thousands of years. George passed those skills on by teaching traditional crafts at schools and cultural centers, and demonstrating techniques that anthropologist Margaret Wheat recorded in *Survival Arts of the Primitive Paiutes*.

Other women of color worked for pay outside the home. Statistically, African-American women were much more likely to work for pay than Euro-American women. They tended to go to work at a younger age, work longer, and a higher percentage continued working after marriage. Relatively few African-Americans lived in early Nevada, but census data indicates that African-American women worked on the Comstock. Eliza Lawson owned property in Virginia City in 1870, and probably took in boarders. Elizabeth Vincent owned a millinery business, one unnamed women was a domestic servant, and several African-American women worked as prostitutes.

Census data also indicates that, with the exception of the Chinese, the various races did not necessarily live and work in segregated areas in the Comstock mining communities. Such was not the case in Carson City, at least regarding the issue of integrated education. In an ad in the *Carson Daily Appeal*, the trustees of the Colored School in Carson City in 1867 advised the community that they had built and paid for the school building. They requested further community support to hire a teacher, but did not specify race or gender of the proposed teacher.

All races and economic classes of women worked more frequently and in a greater variety of jobs in the twentieth century. While some built on traditional "women's work," as teachers and nurses had done, others ventured farther afield. As what was considered appropriate

In 1918, Mary Norton Evans was one of the first women telegraphers on the Western Pacific Railroad. She retired after sixty years of service. (Humboldt Museum)

Effie Mona Mack worked as a university educator and co-authored a textbook. (Las Vegas Library Special Collections)

changed over time, women's jobs changed. Although not the first woman in Nevada to take such a position, Zilpha Hughes Guearo was the postmaster in Mesquite, Nevada from 1909 to 1914. It was a job also held by her father and her brother. With the post office located in the family home, it was convenient employment for a working mother.

Mary Norton Evans's job as telegrapher for the Western Pacific Railroad was less typical for women when she started her career in 1918. One of the first women in Nevada to use this skill, she worked at Jungo station in Humboldt County. Evans continued her job after her marriage in 1923, retiring with sixty years of service. More women were working or continuing to work after marriage in the twentieth century, and although the majority of married women did not work, careers for married women were becoming less rare.

Change was generally slow, but the presence of women in the labor force was sometimes affected by cataclysmic events. The First World War took men out of the work force and on to the frontlines. Women filled in while the boys were "over there." But women's labor was generally viewed as a temporary wartime necessity. Appeals to patriotism put them on the assembly lines, and similar appeals sent them back to the home and domestic tasks at war's end.

World War Two brought women out of the home again, but this time larger numbers remained to work for pay. In 1941, Basic Magnesium built a plant near Las Vegas. Magnesium was a vital ingredient of war materials, and the plant hired thousands of workers during the war. Many of those workers were women, as was the case for defense industries throughout the country. Photos for Basic Magnesium, identified as publicity shots, show smiling women reading mail and lounging in cheerfully decorated rooms, looking more like college coeds than factory workers. Like other factory jobs, the work in munitions plants was both tedious and tiring. And not everyone resided in the comfortable apartments and dormitories provided by BMI. Wartime housing shortages affected southern Nevada, as they did the rest of the country, and many workers lived in whatever shelter was available, including shacks, tents, and cramped travel trailers.

In the decades after the Second World War, job opportunities for women expanded dramatically. Women continued to work in the traditional female occupations—nursing, teaching, and domestic work, among others—but as more and more women worked for

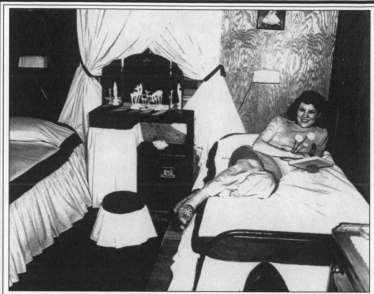

World War II brought war industry to Nevada and labor shortages brought women onto the production line. Basic Magnesium, Inc. provided housing for many of the women who worked at the installation, but ramshackle shelter was a part of wartime shortages. (Henderson Public Library District)

pay, they found a wider range of occupations available than in the past. In Nevada, women workers became more numerous in the casino industry, which expanded rapidly after war's end. Educational and professional opportunities for women also expanded, and, in the post-war decades, increasing numbers of women moved into employment fields previously limited to men.

Nevada's role in the Cold War nuclear industry brought one such woman to this state. Geneva Smith Douglas was a native of Gloucester, Massachusetts, born there in 1932. She attended Mount Holyoke College and received a graduate degree in physiology in 1956. Three years later she moved to Las Vegas as a radiation biologist for the Public Health Service. Nuclear testing at the Nevada Test Site raised environmental concerns, and Douglas became the scientific liaison between Nevada communities and the nuclear industry. She developed an offsite radiation monitoring program, and was active in community issues regarding nuclear testing and public safety. Douglas continued her work with the community and nuclear safety after her retirement in 1985.

Geneva Douglas was one of many Nevada women working for pay, and, increasingly, for personal and professional satisfaction, in recent decades. Women who became scientists, engineers, wildlife biologists, public administrators, and more, stepped completely beyond the boundaries of what was once considered "women's work." The rarity of women working outside the home for pay, as it had been in nineteenth-century Nevada, became the standard in the late twentieth century. With these changes in work for pay, women in Nevada were duplicating changes that were occurring nationally. In the case of casino work as card and craps dealers, Nevada women were breaking new ground.

Mildred Breedlove was a Nevada woman who emerged into the public sphere through her work. Commissioned to write a poem about the state for the 1964 Centennial, Breedlove traveled throughout Nevada to discover the images, events and people who went into her epic poem, *Nevada*. The finished work earned her a nomination for the Nobel Prize for literature and the designation as Nevada's Poet Laureate. One section of Breedlove's poem, describing Nevada landscape and referring to its history, could well be applied to Nevada's working women:

Of late, Nevada wears a party dress;
And Glamour is the topic of the day ---
Her neon glows across the wilderness,
And people come from <u>everywhere</u> to play.
The "Entertainment Center of the World" ---
Where Summer spends the winter --- gay and free ---
However long the desert sands have swirled,
The past is but a page of history.
With our regattas, races, tournaments,
And sports long foreign to the Desert West,
Our sun and sand have gained an eminence
That early settlers never could have guessed.
Our Painted Hills have come into their own ---
A million air-flight passengers may see
A constant change of color tint and tone
That blends in themes of unreality.

Aside from these, nor second in proportion,
Nevada lists, on her "Attractions" chart,
Those works of Nature that defy distortion ---
The timeless values of The Master's Art.

Mildred Breedlove worked as an author and poet. An excerpt of the original manuscript of her 1964 centennial poem is shown here. The poem earned her recognition as Nevada's poet laureate. (Las Vegas Library Special Collections)

Our sun and sand have gained an eminence
That early settlers never could have guessed.
Our painted Hills have come into their own —

Breedlove referred to an entire state, Nevada, when she decreed that the hills "have come into their own." But women had been an important part of building the state that the centennial poem was celebrating. Many women had "come into their own" as they expanded the limits of the domestic sphere in a variety of ways. The emergence into the public sphere of work for pay was an important element in the shifting boundaries of Nevada women's lives.

Jean Ford, 1998

CONCLUSION

A Work In Progress

A work in progress is the phrase Jean Ford used to describe her work in the history of women in Nevada. Through the efforts of fellow members of the Nevada Women's History Project, students in her women's studies and women's history classes, as well as the work of scholars in a variety of fields, knowledge about the history of women in Nevada is gradually growing. The events and personalities of the past can only be determined, however, if the source materials are available. Locating and preserving the documents and artifacts relevant to the past is an important task that Jean and many others have pursued. It is also necessary to make researchers and others interested in the history of Nevada women aware of the sources available to chronicle and explain the past.

The documents in this work, and the women and events, represent diverse types and geographical locations. There are large and small repositories throughout Nevada. A project that Jean Ford began a number of years ago has motivated much of the investigation of women's history by Jean and others. Recently published, *Nevada Women's History: A Guide to Archives and Manuscripts in Nevada Repositories*, provides a wealth of information about places and sources. Some repositories are modest, but can provide both general and specialized information. Others are parts of large institutions, with vast collections and sophisticated technology to guide and assist researchers. Some significant documents are housed in repositories outside Nevada. All types and locations are carefully noted and described in *Nevada Women's History*.

As well as geographic diversity, the documents in this work represent the eclectic types of historical materials that are available in Nevada repositories. Newspapers, published memoirs, and biographies are easily accessible and recognized sources of information. A picture, like the stiff and formal portrait of Sadie Hurst surrounded by male legislators, the more candid shot of Dr. Eliza Cook bathing an infant, or the image of an antiquated automobile carrying women and their suffrage message across the state can convey specific and general information about a person and the past. Equally important are the bits and pieces of the past preserved in Nevada repositories.

Maggie Pulsipher's brief history, written in pencil on lined notebook paper a half century after the fact, provides a personal, and revealing, glimpse into the past. The detail of daily life is often forgotten for its very familiarity. School attendance records from Nelson, Nevada, a town that is no longer on the map, are replete with data that clarify our understanding of the past. The number of children in a class, their ages, even the frequency of the same last names can reveal details about working women, as well as a town and a lifestyle that no longer exists.

The focus of the research in this work has been the public activities of Nevada women. That is, of course, only a small part of a tiny portion of the women in Nevada's past. It is the most logical first step to take in uncovering the history of women in Nevada. Public activities, by nature of their position beyond the privacy of the domestic domain, have generally been better documented. The notice of a meeting printed in the local newspaper is part of the public record and the beginning of historical research. Public documentation builds on that notice. Newspaper coverage of the meeting agenda, program, entertainment, or action taken at that gathering is further documentation. The organization that sponsored the meeting might have membership lists, minutes, newsletters, correspondence, or other materials that contribute to the information available. Members might have kept records of activities, the organization might have sponsored legislation that generated a public record—and so it goes. The paper trail, or photographic record, or oral recollection, or whatever resources are available, forms the basis for historical research. Public activities are the most accessible.

Some events seemed extraordinary at the time, and materials were saved. While a family might save materials about a family member who walks on the moon, it's rare to save grocery receipts or photograph a woman running a vacuum. For these and other reasons, research into the private lives of women of the past can present challenges. But it has been done, and is being done presently. Students from some of Jean Ford's women's studies classes have worked on a project to survey Nevada newspapers in the period marking the last suffrage campaign in 1914-1915. For those years, public information, through newspaper articles, has been well documented, and archived by the Nevada Women's History Project. Such information is a tiny piece of the puzzle, but it is a research interest that has been pursued with beneficial results.

That marks a change in historical attention and scholarship. Until quite recently, with the exception of a very few high profile women, the written history of Nevada has been the history of men and political events. Most histories of Nevada make only brief and passing mention of Nevada women. *Comstock Women* marks a significant beginning to a wider understanding of women's lives in the past. But the contributions that the various chapters and authors make to a better understanding of the activities and impact made by women in an important mining community is only a beginning. In the best tradition of historical inquiry, such works give rise to almost as many questions as are answered. What about other women on the Comstock? What was life like in other mining communities? How did life differ for women on ranches or in small towns? What about the pioneer experience for women?

Casual reading of a newspaper can prompt questions. How did Mrs. Schroeder, the woman who was burned while cleaning clothes in her kitchen in Sparks, perceive her world? The lives and activities of so many women, individuals, types and groups have not yet been researched, nor yet assessed for their role in the events of the past. The history of women of color, of women of various ethnic backgrounds, and of laboring class women—those beyond the better documented lives of Euro-American middle-class women—present challenges for the researcher, and represent a gap in the historical record. Research proceeds on these topics, by a variety of individuals, and the gap is—very slowly—narrowing a bit.

The acquisition and access to the bits and pieces that go into the historical whole of Nevada women are the necessary steps in discovering those events in relation to women's lives. It is evident from the previous chapters that women were important. They made significant contributions to the social structure, political events, economic condition, and quality of life in the past. But precisely what did they do, and why? And how does one go about answering such questions? Documents like those illustrated in this work are part of the answer.

There are others, some discovered and catalogued, some waiting to be found and added to the bits and pieces. Repositories around the state have had the records, manuscripts, photos—the bits and pieces of women's history—in their collections for many years. The problem has been in locating and accessing the materials. The most exciting and useful information is no good unless it can be found and used.

That was a major motivation for the establishment of the Nevada Women's History Project. Much like the members of the clubs established in the nineteenth and twentieth centuries in Nevada, Jean Ford and other like-minded women organized to fill a need in the community. The Nevada Women's History Project is only part of the effort to rescue the history of women from obscurity, and one that has made important and lasting contributions.

As a part of a final examination in some of the classes she has taught, Jean Ford has asked her students to relate how, and if, their perceptions have changed as a result of learning more about Nevada women in history. The response of one student in particular contributes to finding answers for questions about the worth of expanding our knowledge of history in general, and the history of Nevada women specifically:

> I am more acutely aware that what I have considered a woman's experience is colored. . .more reflective of a white woman's experience in a professional environment. . . .I ask more questions now of women who represent minorities, whether racial, economic, or religious; in short, women whose life experiences have taught them different lessons. I specifically seek and create situations in which I can challenge my assumptions and where I have to learn.

Creating precisely such opportunities for expanding knowledge and understanding is part of the legacy that Jean Ford, members of the Nevada Women's History Project, and many historical scholars and researchers have been working to create. Newspaper articles, census records, meeting minutes, photographs, personal letters and memorabilia—every piece that has been saved or recovered builds upon the legacy, and a fuller understanding of our past.

❦ BIBLIOGRAPHY ❦

Selected bibliography for Nevada women's history

Amaral, Anthony. "Idah Meacham Strobridge." *Nevada Historical Society Quarterly* 30 (Summer 1987): 102-110.

Barber, Phyllis. *How I Got Cultured: A Nevada Memoir*. Reno: University of Nevada Press, 1994.

Bennett, Dana R. "Women in Nevada Politics." In *Political History of Nevada, 1996*. 10th ed. Issued by Dean Heller, Secretary of State of Nevada. Carson City, Nevada: State Printing Office, 1996.

Bennion, Sherilyn Cox. "Nellie Verrill Mighels Davis: The `Spirit-of-Things-Achieved.'" *Nevada Historical Society Quarterly* 34 (Fall 1991): 400-413.

Bolton, Maude, and Dorothy Corta. "Maude Bolton: A Pioneer Ranch Woman." *Northeastern Nevada Historical Society Quarterly* (Fall 1987): 71-78.

Brown, Mrs. Hugh. *Lady in Boomtown*. Reno: University of Nevada Press, 1968.

Canfield, Gae Whitney. *Sarah Winnemucca of the Northern Paiutes*. Norman: University of Oklahoma Press, 1983.

Cloud, Barbara. "Images of Women in the Mining Camp Press." *Nevada Historical Society Quarterly* 36 (Fall 1993): 194-207.

Evans, Marguerite Patterson. "Letters from Contact." *Northeastern Nevada Historical Society Quarterly* (Winter 1988): 3-15.

Ford, Jean. *Nevada Women's History: A Guide to Archives and Manuscripts in Nevada Repositories*. Reno: Special Collections Department, University Library, University of Nevada, Reno, 1998.

Ford, Jean, and James W. Hulse. "The First Battle for Woman Suffrage in Nevada: 1869-1871 — Correcting and Expanding the Record." *Nevada Historical Society Quarterly* 38 (Fall 1995): 174-188.

Geuder, Patricia. *Pioneer Women of Nevada*. Carson City: AAUW-DKG
      Publication, 1976.

Glass, Mary Ellen. "Nevada's Lady Lawmakers: The First Half Century."
      Nevada Public Affairs Review 14 (October 1975): 1-18.

Goldman, Marion. *Gold Diggers and Silver Miners: Prostitution and Social
      Life on the Comstock Lode*. Ann Arbor: University of Michigan
      Press, 1981.

Hicks, Connie Noland. "Edna Covert Plummer (1877-1972): First
      Woman District Attorney." *Northeastern Nevada Historical
      Society Quarterly* (Spring 1984)

Hopkins, Sarah Winnemucca. *Life Among the Piutes: Their Wrongs and
      Claims*. Reno: University of Nevada Press, 1994.

Howard, Anne Bail. *The Long Campaign: A Biography of Anne Martin*.
      Reno: University of Nevada Press, 1985.

James, Ronald M. "Women of the Mining West: Virginia City
      Revisited." *Nevada Historical Society Quarterly* 36 (Fall 1993):
      153-177.

James, Ronald M., and C. Elizabeth Raymond, eds. *Comstock Women:
      The Making of a Mining Community*. Reno: University of
      Nevada Press, 1998.

Knudtsen, Molly Flagg. *Here is Our Valley*. Reno: University of Nevada
      Press, 1975.

Lara, Kandi. "Susan Raper: Female Cattle Rustler." *Northeastern Nevada
      Historical Society Quarterly* (Spring 1996): 56-76.

Lewis, Marvin. *Martha and the Doctor: A Frontier Family in Central
      Nevada*. Reno: University of Nevada Press, 1977.

Mathews, Mary McNair. *Ten Years in Nevada, or Life on the Pacific Coast*.
      Lincoln: University of Nebraska Press, 1985.

Olds, Sarah E. *Twenty Miles From a Match: Homesteading in Western
      Nevada*. Reno: University of Nevada Press, 1978.

Patterson, Edna. "Mary Hall: Western Shoshone Basketmaker."
  Northeastern Nevada Historical Society Quarterly 85-4.

Riley, Margaret Ann. "Katherine Lewers." *Nevada Historical Society
  Quarterly* 33 (Summer 1980): 93-97.

Wheat, Margaret M. *Survival Arts of the Primitive Paiutes*. Reno:
  University of Nevada Press, 1967.

Zanjani, Sally Springmeyer. *A Mine of Her Own: Women Prospectors in the
  American West*. Lincoln: University of Nebraska Press, 1997.